Contents

Prologue   Five against Hitler   **6**

PART ONE   THE ROAD TO DICTATORSHIP   9

1 The Young Hitler   **9**
Down-and-out in Vienna   9
Childhood and youth   11
Early political ideas   12
Germany in 1914   14

2 Hitler at War, 1914–19   **16**
Into battle   16
Germany in defeat   18
The Weimar Republic   19
The Treaty of Versailles   20
Germany and the Treaty   22
The world after 1919   23
The German Workers' Party   24

3 The Birth of the Nazi Party, 1920–24   **26**
The 25-point programme   26
Party boss   27
Street fighter   29
Hitler's men   31
The great inflation   32
The beer hall *putsch*   33
Mein Kampf   36

4 Rebuilding the Nazi Party, 1924–29   **38**
Nazism in check?   38
The revival of Germany   40
Re-organising the NSDAP   42

5 The Road to Power, 1929–33   **43**
The Great Depression   43
Government by decree, 1930   44
The Nazi breakthrough, 1930–32   46
Hitler for President   48
The Nazis and the ballot box, 1932–33   50
The crucial weeks, November 1932–January 1933   51

PART TWO   GERMANY UNDER NAZI RULE   53

6 **From Chancellor to Führer**   **53**
   The Nazis in power   53
   Destroying the opposition   55
   'The Night of the Long Knives'   56
   After Hindenburg   57

7 **The Nazi Revolution, 1933–39**   **59**
   The economy   59
   The Jews   63
   The Christian churches   66
   The army   67
   Teenagers in Nazi Germany   68
   School life   70

8 **Nazi Power, 1933–39**   **72**
   The SS and police   72
   The organisation of the SS   73
   Concentration camps   74
   The armed SS (Waffen SS)   76
   The making of SS men   77
   The law courts   79
   Propaganda   80

PART THREE   THE THIRD REICH   82

9 **Germany, Europe and the World, 1933–37**   **82**
   Hitler's view of the world before 1933   82
   Hitler, Italy and Britain, 1933–35   83
   Hitler strengthens his position, 1936–37   86
   The Hossbach Memorandum, November 1937   88

10 **Austria and Czechoslovakia, 1937–39**   **90**
   The Republic of Austria   90
   Preparing for the *Anschluss*   91
   Der Anchluss   92
   The Republic of Czechoslovakia   93
   Case Green   95
   Threats of war   98
   The Munich conference   99
   The final destruction of Czechoslovakia   101

11 **Poland and the 'Phoney War', 1939–40**   **104**
   Britain and Poland   104
   The Polish question   105
   Stalin and Hitler   106
   The Second World War   108
   The 'Phoney War'   109

MODERN TIMES

HITLER AND GERMANY

Second Edition

B. J. Elliott

Longman
London and New York

Acknowledgements

We are grateful to the following for permission to reproduce photographs: Associated Press, page 73; Barnabys Picture Library, page 39; Bildarchiv Preussischer Kulturbesitz, page 137; Giangiacomo Feltrinelli Editore, pages 63, 110; Hulton-Deutsche Collection, pages 29, 86, 93, 103; Robert Hunt Library, page 131; Popperfoto, pages 14, 35, 59, 60; Suddeutscher Verlag, pages 44, 70; Ullstein Bilderdienst, pages 7, 10, 17, 52, 58, 79, 99, 113, 117, 128, 133, 143.

Cover: A commemorative postcard celebrating the unification between Austria and Germany, 13.3.1938. Interfoto Pressebild Agentur.

We are grateful to the author's agent for permission to reproduce extracts from *Looking for Trouble* by Virginia Cowles (pub. Hamish Hamilton Ltd, 1941).

PART FOUR   **HITLER AT WAR**   112

12 **The Years of Victories, 1940–42**   112
    Hitler's attacks on western Europe   112
    The Battle of Britain   114
    The invasion of the USSR   114
    World-wide war   118
    The Battle of Stalingrad   118
    Hitler's war at sea   120

13 **Germany and Europe under Nazi Rule, 1939–45**   121
    The German economy at war   121
    The euthanasia programme   123
    Hitler's war on the Jews   125
    The 'final solution'   127

14 **Resistance**   130
    Resistance outside Germany   130
    Resistance in Germany   132

15 **The Years of Defeats, 1942–45**   135
    Stalingrad and North Africa   135
    The Soviet advance, 1943–45   136
    D-Day   136
    The collapse of Nazi Germany   138

16 **Germany and Europe in 1945**   141
    The toll   141
    The political scene   142
    Nuremburg   142

    Index   144

Prologue

Five against Hitler

The RAF squadron leader

The twin-engined Mosquito light bombers began their long dive. It was nearly 4 p.m. and they had already flown 800 kilometres from Scotland across the North Sea. They had now almost reached the head of the sixty-mile long fjord and their target – Oslo.

Far below them hundreds of men were gathering. They were attending a rally and march-past in honour of their leader, Vidkun Quisling. Suddenly the air-raid sirens blared out and those still outside the building stared skywards. Over a hill to the south-east four dark shapes came swooping down onto the city. Even as they approached, other dark shapes began to fill the sky – FW.190 fighters attacking the invaders with cannon and machine-gun fire. But the counter-attack had come too late; although one Mosquito plunged into the cold waters of Oslo Fjord, the remaining three bore down upon their target. Screaming over the roof-tops at barely 35 metres they unleashed their bombs over the large building where the rally was to begin. As he climbed away high above the city, Squadron Leader D.A.G. Parry, DFC, the flight commander, looked back and saw a great cloud of red dust and smoke. He then turned and with his two companions headed back to Scotland.

The Jewish teenager

In another European city, 1000 kilometres to the south-west of Oslo, two families were sitting down to Sunday dinner. They were in a third-floor room at the rear of a large house. The house stood by a canal on Prinsengracht, a street in Amsterdam. The mother of one of the families spoke to the younger daughter of the other family:

'Come along, Anne, have a few more vegetables.'
'No thank you, Mrs Van Daan, I have plenty of potatoes.'
'Vegetables are good for you, your mother says so too.

A conversation you might hear at a million Sunday dinner tables; but this was not a typical Sunday dinner for the group sitting round the table. For two-and-a-half months they had been living in two rooms shut off from the world by a secret door. They would remain hidden for another two years until they were betrayed. The girl who disliked vegetables was Anne Frank. She was thirteen years old and, like the other six people in the room, was a Jew.

The Red Army sergeant

Several hours later a Russian sergeant scribbled on a piece of paper: 'House captured. Await further orders.' Crouching amongst the rubble of his prize already littered with his own and enemy dead, the sergeant, Jacob Pavlov, knew nothing of Anne Frank's house 2700 kilometres away. But he did know an attempt would be made to recapture his house. For sixty-two days Pavlov and his men held the house in the face of one vicious attack after another. Pavlov's house was in Stalingrad.

German soldiers in Stalingrad

The US Navy lieutenant

Far out in the South Atlantic a slight mist had risen over a calm sea. As the mist increased it had become mixed with smoke from a raging fire. The fire was raging aboard a ship, the *S. S. Stephen Hopkins*, bound from South Africa to the Caribbean. For twenty minutes shells and machine-gun bullets had been crashing against it. At last with the main boiler burst, the deckhouse ablaze and the radio shot away, the Captain had given the order – 'Abandon ship'.

The *Stephen Hopkins* was going down fighting. As soon as the first shell had struck, Lieutenant Kenneth M. Willett, commander of the guard, had leapt to man the gun. Shrapnel had torn a wound in his stomach. In spite of this Lt. Willett fired off most of his thirty-five shells at his attackers. When his ammunition store had been blown up he had staggered down to the main deck to help to launch the life-rafts.

The Yugoslav partisan

Hidden in the mountains of southern Yugoslavia, an army of 150,000 men and women prepared to fight. They wore no uniforms and they came from different ethnic groups. But they were determined, disciplined and under the command of Communist Party officials. Their leader was Josip Broz (1892–1980), a veteran of the First World War and the Russian Civil War. Since 1937, when a secret agent of the Yugoslav Communist Party, he had been known as 'Tito'. He knew that soon a ferocious attempt would be made to destroy his army. For Tito was a resistance leader, the greatest and most successful of the Second World War, and his army were partisans.

September 1942

Thus passed a few hours in the lives of five people. It was the last weekend of September 1942. Although separated by thousands of kilometres, these five were united in a fight. They were fighting to destroy a hideous evil which had gripped Europe: the empire of Adolf Hitler.

From the Volga to the Atlantic and from the Arctic Circle to the Sahara the forces of this one man ruled supreme. Ten million soldiers from Germany, Italy and eastern Europe had marched in triumph through Paris, Brussels, Copenhagen, Warsaw, Athens and Kiev. In the factories and upon the farms of Germany untold millions slaved and died to supply his armies. In the dark alleys of Amsterdam and Belgrade and a hundred other cities men and women disappeared for ever into the night and fog. On the desolate plains of Poland a thousand victims daily gasped and screamed as a silent death struck them.

Such was Europe in September 1942.

Nations against Hitler

Squadron Leader Parry attacked that building in Oslo because it was the Norwegian headquarters of the Gestapo. The men meeting there were traitors who had helped in the conquest of their own country.

Anne Frank hid in Amsterdam because Jews from all parts of Europe were slaughtered every day in Poland. Anne was betrayed and died shortly before her sixteenth birthday, but her diary has survived.

Sergeant Pavlov fought grimly in Stalingrad because it was in Russia that most of the German army was fighting in a savage bloodbath. Stalingrad had become its very centre and would cost a quarter of a million lives in less than half a year.

Lieutenant Willett died defending his ship against German merchant raiders because on Hitler's orders every Allied ship was to be sunk on sight – ships which were the very lifelines of the Allied war effort.

Tito was engaged in a great fight to free his country from its German and Italian invaders. Furthermore, he was determined that after victory, Yugoslavia was not going to be a monarchy again as it had been from 1919–41. He was going to establish a communist government. The Germans were never successful in defeating Tito. In 1945 he became President of Yugoslavia and remained in office until his death in 1980.

Five against Hitler. Who was this man Hitler? What forces in his childhood, upbringing or adult life had fashioned such a character? How had this man risen to be Lord of Germany? How had he been able to trample underfoot a score of European nations and defy for a while the world's greatest powers? To begin finding the answers to these and other related questions we must, from 1942, put the clock back to 1909 and move to yet another great European city – Vienna.

PART ONE

THE ROAD TO DICTATORSHIP

1
The Young Hitler, 1889–1914

Down-and-out in Vienna

The Austro-Hungarian Empire

In 1909 Vienna was already a very large city with a population of 2 million. It was the capital of the Austro-Hungarian Empire. This Empire included not only today's Austria and Hungary but also large parts of modern Yugoslavia, Czechoslovakia, Poland and Romania. It was a multi-national Empire with a population of almost 50 million. The German-speaking Austrians, with 12 million, were the largest nation. There were more than 10 million Magyars, or Hungarians, 6.5 million Czechs and 5 million Poles. There were other nationalities also.

With so many different nations in one Empire there were as many different ideas about its future. The Hungarians, who had had some self-rule since 1867 with their own parliament in Budapest, wanted complete independence. The Czechs and Poles wanted their own nation states. The Slavs wanted to join Serbia. Many German Austrians wanted to join the German Empire under Kaiser William II.

Anti-semitism

Internal migration within the Empire had created populations of mixed nationality everywhere. It was impossible to be fair to everyone in the choice of language. For example, the Czechs wanted their language, not German, as the official language in their own areas. Amongst these mixed populations there was a lot of mistrust and racial hatred. The particular hatred and jealousy known as anti-semitism was felt towards the Jews who lived in large numbers in Vienna and Budapest. Many, but by no means all, had become rich.

The ruling nations of the Empire were the German-speaking Austrians and the Hungarian-speaking Magyars. To keep control of this situation, which seemed to threaten the break-up of the Empire, large police forces were employed. The people did not have as many civil rights, such as voting, as did most of the male populations of Britain, France and the USA.

The city

Vienna was not only large and important, it was also, at least in parts, very beautiful. In the 1850s many fine buildings had been put up along the circular Ringstrasse. The richest and most important people of the Empire lived there – officers, officials, bankers, ambassadors, dukes

The glory of imperial Vienna on the sixtieth anniversary of the Emperor's reign

and princes. Most important of all was the Emperor himself. This was Franz-Josef II, almost eighty years of age in 1909, who had ruled since 1848 and died in 1916. Franz-Josef knew about the major problems of his Empire but instead of making changes he did the opposite. He tried to rule his Empire as it had been ruled in his youth. The result was even more hatred, anger, tension and secret plotting.

Poverty

Keeping things as they were meant for most poor people there was little hope of a better life. Vienna in particular was full of poor people. The population of the city had been growing much faster than houses and flats could be built. Some crowded ten or more to a room. Others slept in 'warming rooms', the men on benches, the women and children on the floor. Some even slept in the city's sewers for warmth and shelter. For single men there were dosshouses or 'Homes for Men'.

The tramp

In the Meidling district in the south west of Vienna a tramp named Rheinhold Hanisch arrived at one of these homes on a cold October night in 1909. He found an empty bed. Then he noticed the man next to him wearing only an old pair of trousers. The man's clothes were being cleaned of lice which he had picked up whilst sleeping rough. Hanisch asked his name – 'Adolf Hitler' was the reply.

So here was the future ruler of Germany and conqueror of Europe. He was broke, unemployed, homeless, half-starved and in need of a bath and some clean clothes. He was then twenty years of age.

Hitler commented on the rich and poor in pre-1914 Vienna, in a book he wrote in 1924 called *Mein Kampf*, which means 'My Struggle':

'Dazzling riches and loathsome destitution were intermingled in contrast ... Beside a horde of military officers of high rank, State officials, artistes and scientists, there was the still vaster horde of workers ... Thousands of unemployed loitered in front of the palaces on the Ring Strasse ... the homeless huddled together in the murk and filth of the canals ... The Vienna manual labourers lived in surroundings of appalling misery. I shudder even today when I think of the woeful dens in which people dwelt, the night shelters and the slums.'

Adolf Hitler, *Mein Kampf*, 1924

Childhood and youth

Parents

Hitler was not a native of Vienna nor did he come from a poor family. He was born on 20 April 1889 in Braunau-am-Inn, a small village on the Austrian-German border. Hitler's father, Alois, was the customs officer there earning the equivalent of £100 a year, twice the wage of a factory worker. Alois Hitler was illegitimate at birth. His mother Maria Ann Schicklegruber was a housemaid. Five years later she married Johann Heidler. The name was spelt Hitler after Heidler's death.

Alois was fifty-two when Adolf was born. His mother, Klara, was twenty-nine. Alois and Klara had five children but only Adolf and his sister Paula (b. 1896) survived early childhood. It was not surprising that his mother worried about his health.

At school

During Hitler's childhood the family moved houses several times, because of his father's job. In April 1895 Alois bought a house and some land and retired from the customs to farm and keep hens. Meanwhile the young Hitler started primary school. He did very well, gaining high marks.

Alois didn't settle down and the family made more moves. In September 1900 Hitler started at the secondary technical school at Linz. Apart from gymnastics at which he was graded 'excellent' he did well only in drawing, history and geography. He found difficulty with German, maths and science and he hated French.

Hitler clearly did best in subjects which required imagination. He also enjoyed make-believe games, particularly with younger children. He played cowboys and Indians and Boers v. Britons. (The Anglo-Boer War of 1899–1902 made Britain very unpopular in Europe.)

The bad school reports made Hitler's relationship with his father much worse. Alois wanted his son to become a customs officer but Hitler had other ideas. Later he said he did badly at school deliberately so he wouldn't be able to become a customs officer.

This is Hitler's own description of himself as a ten-year-old:

'I spent a good deal of time scampering about in the open on the long road from school, and mixing up with some of the toughest of boys ... All this tended to make me quite the reverse of a stay-at-home ... I think that an inborn talent for speaking now began to develop and take shape during the more or less strenuous arguments which I used to have with my comrades. I had become a juvenile ringleader who learned well and easily at school but was rather difficult to manage.'

Mein Kampf, 1924

After school

The difficulty with his father ended in 1903 when Alois died. This left Hitler, at fourteen, the oldest male in the household. He was able then to behave as he wished. So after a barely satisfactory report (with the exception of gymnastics and free-hand drawing, both 'excellent') in September 1905 he left school. The reason given was ill-health.

Hitler's mother agreed he could apply to enter the Vienna Academy of Fine Arts. Meanwhile he read a great deal, made sketches, wandered the streets of Linz and visited museums and the cinema. Early in 1907 his mother was found to have cancer. Despite the surgical removal of one breast the tumour spread and within a year the eighteen-year-old Adolf Hitler was an orphan.

Early political ideas

In Vienna

During his mother's final illness, Hitler had applied unsuccessfully to enter the Vienna Academy of Fine Arts. He failed to get in in 1908 and in 1910 also. This was not surprising. Only 28 out of 113 applicants were accepted. Hitler was not a great artist. His best work was copying and he preferred drawing buildings to people or nature.

Despite his rejection by the Academy, he returned to Vienna after his mother's funeral. She had left him enough money to rent a cheap room. This he shared with August Kubizek, who later, in 1953, wrote a book about their friendship. Hitler slept late and spent his days reading, sketching and visiting public buildings. He loved to visit the opera but he could not afford a seat and had to go in the standing area.

Political views

He once sat in the public gallery of the Austrian parliament. There he looked down on deputies (MPs) holding noisy debates, and often speaking in one of the Slav languages used in their country within the Austrian empire. Later he described the scene and drew his own conclusions about parliamentary democracy:

'The intellectual level of the debate was quite low. Sometimes the debaters did not make themselves intelligible at all. Several of those present did not speak German but only their slav vernaculars or dialects . . . A turbulent mass of people all gesticulating and bawling against one another, with a pathetic old man shaking his bell and making frantic efforts to call the House to a sense of its dignity . . . I could not help laughing . . . Democracy as practised in Western Europe today is the forerunner of Marxism. In fact the latter would not be conceivable without the former . . . By the introduction of parliamentarianism democracy produced an abortion of filth and fire.'

Mein Kampf, 1924

With no job and no dole or social security in Austria, Hitler began to run short of money. In 1909 this drove him into the dosshouse. Later his situation improved. He drew postcards, sketches and advertisement posters which he sold and he also got help from an aunt. When she died she left him money equal to three years' wages for a labourer.

Hitler's anti-semitism

Life in Vienna was hard for the would-be artist. He found it difficult to keep himself fed, clothed and sheltered. He also noticed that many people around him were much better off than him. These were not only the 'German' Austrians but Magyars, Czechs, Italians, Poles – and also Jews. However, Hitler was probably no more anti-semitic than most people in Vienna at first. Two of his best friends were Jews. His mother had been treated by a Jewish doctor during her last illness and Hitler had been very grateful for his efforts. He accepted help from Jewish charities. But there are strong hints that his attitude was changing. Hitler read a great deal of anti-semitic writings including *Deutsches Volksblatt*, a Viennese paper which was full of such stuff. Much later Hitler claimed his hatred for the Jews had started at this time.

In *Mein Kampf* Hitler described how his feelings about Jews grew, stage by stage, in Vienna:

> 'Once, when passing through the Inner City I suddenly encountered a phenomenon in a long caftan and wearing black sidelocks. My first thought was: Is this a Jew? They certainly didn't have this appearance in Linz. I watched the man stealthily and cautiously . . . the question shaped itself in my brain: Is this a German?'
> (Later)
> 'Wherever I now went I saw Jews and the more I saw of them the more strikingly and clearly they stood out as a different people.'
> (Later)
> 'Was there any shady undertaking, any form of foulness, especially in cultural life in which at least one Jew did not participate?'
> (Later)
> 'One fact became evident to me. It was that this alien race held in its hands the leadership of the Social Democratic Party. I was happy to know for certain that the Jew was not a German.'
>
> *Mein Kampf*, 1924

Munich

Hitler's interest in politics and history was the result of his schooling, his vast reading and his dislike of the Austro-Hungarian Empire. By contrast he was strongly attracted to Germany. He believed all 'Germans' (such as the German-speaking Austrians) should be citizens of the German Empire. So on 24 May 1913 Hitler left Vienna and went to live in Munich. This was the capital city of the Kingdom of Bavaria and part of the German Empire. He found lodgings, began painting and sketching and trying to sell the results, which was very difficult in Munich. Early in 1914 he received an order from the Austrian army to report for military service. When he arrived he was given a medical examination and found unfit for service.

Munich as Hitler would have seen it in 1913

The soldier

Hitler returned immediately to Munich. When World War I broke out a few months later Hitler shared in the excitement and nationalist feelings which swept through Europe's capitals. On 16 August 1914 he was accepted into the 16th Bavarian Reserve Infantry Regiment and served continuously for almost six years.

Germany in 1914

The Empire

At the outbreak of the First World War, the German Empire had existed for forty-three years. It had been formed immediately after the successful war against France in 1870–1. It was a federal Empire consisting of twenty-six states. The largest and most important were the Kingdoms of Prussia (capital, Berlin) and Bavaria. The German Emperor was Kaiser William II (1888–1918) who was also King of Prussia. He appointed the Chancellor, who was head of the government, and other ministers. The Diet, or Parliament, had two houses: the Bundesrat and the Reichstag. Seven major political parties had won seats in these Houses in the 1912 election. The socialists (SPD) with 112 seats were the largest, followed by the Catholic Centre Party with 91. In addition there were assemblies or Diets in most of the twenty-six states and territories of the Empire.

Military power

Despite the growth of the socialist party, the most powerful and important people in Germany were the nobles (Junkers) and army officers. Many nobles, as well as owning large estates, were also army officers. By 1913 Germany had the best equipped and trained army in the world, if not quite the largest. Germany was able to pay for this powerful army because of its highly successful economy. It had become the world's second greatest industrial power after the USA. Germany had overtaken Britain around 1900 and was particularly successful in steel, chemicals, electrical goods, machine tools and motors.

Rivalry with Britain

The rise of German industrial power worried Britain which was still the most successful trading nation. Even more worrying to Britain had been Germany's decision to build a large navy. By 1910 Britain and Germany were each trying desperately to build the largest fleet of the new dreadnought battleships. If Germany succeeded, the British believed their Empire would be lost. If Germany failed, the Germans believed they would never become a true world power.

Britain and Germany also saw each other as likely enemies because of the system of military alliances in Europe. The German and Austro-Hungarian Empires had been allies since 1879 and Italy had joined them in a Triple Alliance in 1882. Bismarck, the German Chancellor, had tried to keep on friendly terms with Russia also. However, in 1893, after Bismarck's dismissal, Russia and France had signed an alliance.

The Triple Entente

Britain remained isolated while these European alliances were being built. She was more concerned with protecting her world-wide empire. In 1902 she signed a treaty with Japan whose power was growing in the Far East. With Japan as an ally, Britain felt it was safer to give attention to Europe. By 1904 she had reached a 'friendly under-standing', or *entente cordiale*, with France. In 1907 this became the 'Triple Entente' when Britain came to an agreement with Russia about some long-running disagreements, especially in Afghanistan, which lay between Russia and Britain's empire in India. Russia was now able to move troops away from its Asian borders in the south and keep them in European Russia.

The trenches

The Franco-Russian Alliance and the Triple Entente meant that, in a major war, Germany would have to split her forces to fight Russia in the east and France in the west. Unless she won a quick victory on one front she would be in serious difficulty. In August the German armies crossed into France and thrust towards Paris. They seemed about to win their quick victory but they were held outside the French capital at the Battle of the Marne. The two sides then dug in to face each other from trenches. Failure to win victory in the west meant that Germany could not take advantage of her crushing defeat of the Russian armies at the Battle of Tannenburg in the east. The war would now be won by whichever side managed to exhaust the other on the Western Front. This is where Hitler spent the next four years.

2
Hitler at War 1914–19

Into battle

The western Front

On 7 October 1914 after nearly two months training, Hitler and his regiment marched 110 kilometres west of Munich for intensive battle training. Then they left by train for the western front and the first battle of Ypres. The regiment·suffered heavy casualties and Hitler gained his first decoration, the Iron Cross 2nd class.

Soon Hitler was living and fighting in the trenches. These stretched for 700 kilometres from the Belgian coast to Switzerland. Month after month British, French, German and colonial troops charged their enemies' trenches. They were killed and wounded by machine guns fired by the defenders. Others were killed by the shells which burst as they carried heavy equipment across a no-man's-land covered with shell holes, barbed wire and often thick mud.

The dispatch runner

Hitler may not have taken part in any bayonet charges at the enemy lines but he had a job almost as dangerous. He was a dispatch runner carrying messages between the regimental headquarters and the trenches. Casualties amongst runners were very high. In most respects Hitler was a very good soldier. He carried out his duties reliably and courageously. He never left a wounded comrade or tried to be excused duties. He wouldn't accept extra food from other soldiers. Unlike them, he received no parcels from home and could not repay the favour. He was regarded, not surprisingly, as 'a bit peculiar'. He talked only politics or of the evils of smoking and drinking. He never complained. He continued to paint and sketch and never asked for leave to go home for a few days. He was also very lucky – he fought in the great battle of the Somme against the British in 1916 and received only one shrapnel wound in the leg.

In Munich

Hitler found himself recovering in a Berlin hospital. Later he was posted to Munich. He was upset by what he saw there. The Allied naval blockade of the central powers and the decline in Germany's own production had created serious food shortages. People were cold and

A German field-dressing post behind the front during the battle of the Somme

hungry and they complained a lot. Other people had got hold of supplies and were selling them on the black market at high prices. Hitler was disgusted by both the complaints and by the black marketeers. Compared with the hardships of front line soldiers they had little to complain about. Later, he claimed it was at this time he first realised fully who was behind Germany's troubles – the Jews. Everywhere he went in Munich, he said, he saw young Jewish men who were avoiding military service. He believed that the Jews were strengthening their position in German life by making big profits from the War.

Queueing for rationed potatoes in Berlin, 1917

**At the front
again**

Hitler was pleased to be sent back to his regiment at the front. He was promoted to lance-corporal and continued his work as a runner. The regiment was soon back in action and having to face new weapons, bombers and tanks. In July 1917 it suffered a ten-day artillary bombardment. Still Hitler survived. Later in 1917 he went on leave for the first time. By this time the food shortage in Germany was desperate. Most people were getting only about one-third of what they really needed. Soldiers and civilians began to eat dogs and cats and to steal food. By early 1918 strikes and hunger marches began in Austria-Hungary and spread to Germany.

**The July
offensive**

However, in March 1918 Germany was able to force Lenin and the Bolsheviks in Russia to accept a harsh peace treaty. This left Germany free to start transferring more troops to the western front. Most of the German army was then certain it could win the War. In July, massive attacks were made on the western front, where American troops were arriving. In one action Hitler captured four French soldiers and was awarded the Iron Cross, 1st class. It was pinned on his chest by Lt. Hugo Guttman, a Jew! By the end of the war he had been awarded six medals but despite his long, loyal service he never rose beyond the rank of corporal. This was partly because of his job and partly because he was not considered to be a 'natural leader'.

However, despite the bravery of the German army the attacks failed. In August the western Allies went onto the attack. The Germans were soon retreating and now they could never hope to win. In particular because thousands more fresh American troops were arriving in France.

Armistice

On 14 October Hitler was blinded in a mustard gas attack. His eyes were not permanently damaged but his throat and speech were. By the time he was released from hospital five weeks later, the German government had requested and been given a cease-fire on Armistice Day, 11 November 1918. But revolution had broken out in Germany. Kaiser William II had given up his throne and fled to neutral Holland.

Hitler later described his distress at hearing of the Armistice:

'So it had all been in vain. In vain all the sacrifices and privations, in vain the hunger and thirst for endless months, in vain those hours that we stuck to our posts though the fear of death gripped our souls and in vain the death of two millions who fell discharging that duty.'

Mein Kampf, 1924

Germany in defeat

Hitler learned of Germany's fall while in hospital. He wrote later:

'I knew all was lost. Only fools, liars and criminals could hope on the mercy of the enemy. In these nights hatred grew in me, hatred for those responsible for this deed. In the days that followed, my own fate became known to me . . . I decided to go into politics.'

Revolution

The people of Germany had united in 1914 to fight the Allies. By 1918 hunger and defeat had shattered this unity. Germany's defeat came as a great shock to most people. For years the news had spoken only of the prospect of certain victory. Early in November sailors at Kiel on the Baltic coast mutinied. After years blockaded in port they were upset by a rumour of a planned suicide attack on the British fleet. This munity led to the setting up of Workers' and Soldiers' Councils modelled on those in Soviet Russia. Other German cities followed Kiel's example. The German Chancellor, Prince Max, handed over his office to the socialist leader Frederick Ebert. On 9 November he declared Germany a republic.

Civil war

Ebert's government was in difficulties. The communists wanted the state to take over all industry (as in Russia) and abolish the army. The army was returning home and many senior officers planned to destroy the revolution and seize power. Ebert made an agreement with General Groener, the army commander. Groener would support the government and keep order with his troops. Ebert would support the army and keep it intact. He had recognised that the power of his government depended on the army.

The Spartakists

In December this agreement was put to the test. From all parts of Germany groups of left-wing socialists and communists came to Berlin. They had many things to discuss including the abolition of the army. Then they attacked the Chancellory building and Ebert had to call on the army for help. Early in the New Year of 1919 the army, assisted by the *Freikorps* (right-wing 'irregular' ex-soldiers), attacked the rebels. Led by Karl Liebknecht and Rosa Luxemburg, the Spartakists, as the rebels called themselves, were crushed in savage fighting. The two leaders were captured and shot.

Revolution in Bavaria

In Bavaria, also, a revolution had taken place. The Social Democrat Party (SPD) led by Kurt Eisner had declared Bavaria a republic and taken over the government. The SPD was heavily defeated in state elections and a month later in February 1919 Eisner was assassinated.

In the confusion that followed, the Social Democrats, the Independent Socialists and the Communists all declared themselves to be the Bavarian government. As in Berlin the army and the *Freikorps* moved in. For nine days Munich was the centre of the fighting. Over 500 people were killed, many not involved in the struggle. The army did not allow the Social Democrats to hold on to power as they had in Berlin. Instead it backed a right-wing government which took over the new Republic of Bavaria.

The Weimar Republic

First elections

In the midst of this civil war the Socialist government, as promised, called a general election. They themselves won 165 out of 423 seats,

39 per cent of the total. This meant that to govern Germany the Socialists would require the support of other parties.

The National Assembly met in neither Berlin nor Munich, the rival centres of power. The meeting place was Weimar, a small town about 300 kilometres south-west of Berlin. The town gave its name to the Weimar Republic by which Germany from 1919–1933 is usually known. The National Assembly had three tasks: first to create a lawfully elected government; second to make peace with the Allies (the Armistice was only a cease-fire); and third to create a constitution for the Republic which would lay down how Germany was to be governed.

Chancellor Scheidemann

Friedrich Ebert was elected President of Germany by a majority of 73 per cent of the deputies of the Assembly. Philipp Scheidemann became the first Chancellor. However, Scheidemann had to bring other parties into the government because of the lack of a socialist majority. Coalition government worked fairly well as long as the democratic parties held the majority. Even so, there was a change of government once a year on average during the Republic's lifetime.

The Treaty of Versailles, 1919

Three leaders

Having got rid of the Kaiser and established a democratic government, the National Assembly thought that the Allies might treat Germany leniently. This was not the case.

The Peace Conference opened in Paris in January 1919, the same month as the German elections. It was a meeting of the victorious Allies to decide on the terms of the treaties they would make Germany and their other defeated enemies sign. President Wilson of the USA, President Georges Clemenceau of France, and Prime Minister David Lloyd George of Great Britain were the most important delegates. Clemenceau was the chairman but Wilson's 'fourteen points' formed the basis for the discussions. Wilson believed that war could be outlawed by a new international organization, the League of Nations. Lloyd George did not think this was the most important issue. Clemenceau believed that peace could be kept only by disarming Germany, whilst the Western Allies remained militarily strong.

War guilt

As the delegates discussed the terms of the Treaty, the general opinion became clear: that Germany should be declared guilty of aggressive war, punished and weakened economically and militarily. If the Treaty succeeded in doing this it would change the balance of power in Europe. Once again France would become Europe's major power because Britain's interests lay outside Europe and Russia was in an appalling situation. Civil war had broken out there and the Western Allies had begun sending troops into Russia to help the anti-Bolsheviks.

The Treaty terms

There were over 400 articles in the Treaty. The most important were:

Armed forces The German Army was to be cut and kept to 100,000

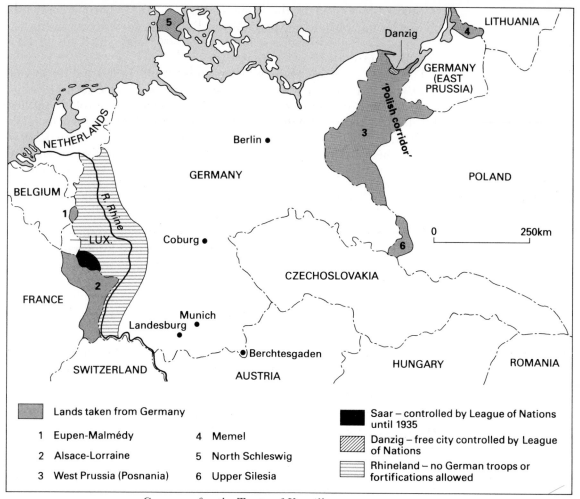

Germany after the Treaty of Versailles

men. Germany was not to be allowed to possess or build military aircraft, tanks, submarines or more than six battleships. German soldiers had to serve for twelve years so that a pool of trained reserves could not be built by having large numbers spend two or three years each in the army.

European territories The Allies had few difficulties in making terms about the western frontiers. Germany was made to return Alsace and Lorraine which she had seized from France in 1871. The Saarland, an important industrial area, was to be administered by the League of Nations for fifteen years. Eupen-Malmédy was given to Belgium and North Schleswig to Denmark.

The Treaty makers had more problems in the east. They gave the Poles a national home after 150 years when their territory had been divided first between the Russian, Austrian and German empires. One result of this long period under foreign domination was that Poles and

Germans often lived in the same districts, so the reborn Poland had many Germans inside her boundaries. Poland needed access to the sea which was arranged by giving her a corridor of land which cut off East Prussia from the rest of Germany.

The hope of many Germans that they would be all united in one state was shattered by the decisions on Austria and Czechoslovakia. Austria lost her empire and became a small state of 7 million people. Almost all were Germans but Austria was forbidden to make a union, or *anschluss*, with Germany. Czechoslovakia was created out of part of the old Austro-Hungarian Empire. The west and south-western districts made up the Sudetenland where a majority were German.

Overseas empire Germany had to surrender all colonies in Africa, China and the Pacific. They were taken over by the Allies.

War guilt Germany and her allies had to accept full responsibility for the war and all the damage caused. The Kaiser and hundreds of other Germans, including Hindenburg, were to be tried as war criminals but these trials never took place. The amount to be paid in damages by Germany was finally settled at £6.6 billion (equal to £140 billion in 1990). France, Belgium and Britain were to receive most of this.

The Rhineland demilitarised As a guarantee against more attacks on France, the Germans had to remove all troops and military positions from the east bank of the Rhine. No German troops could be stationed within fifty kilometres of the river for the next thirty years.

Germany and the Treaty

The National Assembly in Weimar had known of the terms of the Treaty for several weeks before the signing was to take place. On 12 May 1919 the main party leaders had, in turn, condemned the Treaty. 'A terrible and murderous attack' said Chancellor Scheidemann.

The Treaty signed

No amount of angry speeches could change the fact that Germany had to sign. The Allies' navies had blockaded German ports since Autumn 1918 to prevent food and raw materials entering. They would not lift the blockade until the Treaty was signed. If Germany had refused, an Allied invasion of Germany could have followed. Eventually, by a vote of 237 to 138, the deputies agreed to sign.

On 28 June the German delegates arrived at the Palace of Versailles outside Paris for the ceremony. This took place in the Hall of Mirrors where less than fifty years before, William I was proclaimed Emperor of Germany after the defeat of France. For France in June 1919 the Treaty was sweet revenge.

Stab in the back

The *Deutsche Zeitung* (German News), a right-wing paper, spoke for a great many Germans, when on the morning of the signing it carried an angry front-page message:

> ## Vengeance! German Nation!
>
> 'Today in the Hall of Mirrors in Versailles the disgraceful Treaty is being signed. Do not forget it! The German people will with unceasing labour press forward to reconquer the place amongst nations to which it is entitled. Then will come vengeance for the shame of 1919 '

The new democratic government of Germany was accused of having betrayed the country. It was these politicians who had signed the Armistice and signed the Peace Treaty. Meanwhile the German Army had remained undefeated and outside the borders of Germany. In other words, said the generals and others, the army had been 'stabbed in the back' by the politicians. Hitler agreed fully with this accusation. He repeated it frequently.

In 1919 the Western powers, both politicians and people, believed that Germany alone was guilty of starting the war. The Treaty aimed to weaken Germany. Yet the task of enforcing it was left mainly to the Germans themselves. They had to collect the immense reparations payments and hand them over to the Allies. They had to reduce their armed forces and get rid of the forbidden weapons. However German firms such as Krupps continued secretly to make weapons in Germany and through companies they owned in other European countries.

The world after 1919

Despite the punishment clauses, Germany could easily become again the strongest European power. Russia had collapsed into civil war and chaos. Both Britain and France had smaller populations and industrial production. The Western powers realised this but hoped that Germany could be held in check by the League of Nations and by the new map of Europe they had drawn in the Treaty of Versailles and the other treaties they had forced Austria-Hungary and the Ottoman (Turkish) Empire to sign. Drawing the new map had also been made much easier by the fact that Russia's new Bolshevik government was too troubled by civil war to hold on to some lands on their western frontiers.

The new Europe

There was now a belt of new countries starting with Finland, Poland and the Baltic States (Estonia, Latvia and Lithuania) in the north and running through Hungary, Czechoslovakia and a larger Romania down into Yugoslavia. The Paris peacemakers had set out to create new states for the nationalities who had lived under the empires which collapsed as a result of the war: the German, Russian, Austro-Hungarian and Turkish. France saw them in another way. They were a 'cordon sanitaire', or security line, of states which would band with each other and with France to prevent Germany expanding. There were weaknesses in this thinking. One was that Russia had lost parts of Poland

and Romania as well as the Baltic states from her pre-war empire so she would not back their efforts to stay independent. The other was that the new states contained a mixture of nationalities. For instance Poland, Germany and Hungary could all claim that people of their nation had been drawn into Czechoslovakia.

Britain and France

There were problems, too, for the victorious powers themselves. France had suffered war deaths of 1.5 million, mostly young men. In a future war there might be a shortage of soldiers as well as workers. Britain's war deaths were high but only about half of those of France. France's greatest concern was the possibility of a new threat from Germany but Britain did not share this. Her biggest problem was the loss of much of her leading position in world trade and industry which led to problems of unemployment and industrial unrest. The war had actually increased her empire with new lands to run as League mandates in the Middle East and Africa; her political leaders wanted, therefore, to avoid involvement in European problems.

The USA

Only the USA emerged richer and stronger. Her industrial production had expanded rapidly to supply Britain and France. They now owed America about £2 billion (equal to about £40 billion in 1990) for armaments and raw materials. These debts were to be repaid to the USA with the money which came to Britain and France from German reparations. By 1919, the USA was much the richest and strongest power in the world. However, her political leaders would not use this strength to keep the peace in Europe. Congress rejected joining the League of Nations which their President had been so keen to set up.

The German Workers' Party

Hitler had left hospital on 21 November 1918 having recovered his sight. He was ordered back to Munich. He was not involved in the events early in 1919 leading to the overthrow of Eisner's socialist government in Bavaria. Part of this time he spent guarding French and Russian prisoners of war. Along with other soldiers he was arrested by *Freikorps* men when they seized Munich in May 1919. Hitler was recognised by officers who knew of his war record and he was released unharmed.

The political agent

During the summer he attended political training courses organised by the army to develop anti-communist attitudes in selected officers and men. In Hitler these attitudes existed already, and he now had a hatred of the Jews who were, he believed, also the world's leading communists. Hitler impressed his instructors with his ability to argue and to make speeches. He was posted as a political agent to a special army unit in Munich commanded by Captain Karl Mayr. Hitler's task was to investigate the activities of some of the fifty small political groups in the city. These groups were supported by money from Ger-

3
The Birth of the Nazi Party 1920–24

The 25-point programme

German Workers' Party	Munich
Munich Group	2 December 1919

We hereby request you to be sure to attend a
meeting
to take place on Wednesday 10 December 1919
at 7 p.m. in the German Reich Tavern,
143 Dachauer Street (tram stop 24 Lori Street)

Speaker: Mr Hittler on 'Germany in her
deepest humiliation'.

This invitation serves as a ticket. The hall
is heated.

>
> The Committee
> A. Josef Mayer
> First Secretary 10/3 Andräs St.

**Party
re-organisation**

This is a translation (with Hitler's name spelt as it appeared) of the earliest notice still in existence of a political meeting addressed by Hitler. For Hitler's first tactic was to build up the membership by holding larger meetings. Bigger audiences also meant larger collections. The money was then used to advertise the next meeting. When he joined the group Hitler thought it was only a debating society. By the end of 1919 he had re-organised it into a political party. Drexler supported Hitler's ideas and they met frequently to plan their programme.

Together they put together the Party's Manifesto which consisted of twenty-five basic ideas. Hitler wanted to make these public quickly at a big meeting. This was arranged for 24 February 1920 at the Hofbrauhaus in Munich.

In the Hofbrauhaus

Posters and leaflets were distributed all over Munich. When Hitler entered the hall at 7.15 p.m. it was packed with almost 2000 people. Probably more than half were communists and socialists who were hostile to the new and growing party. After a 'warm-up' speaker, Hitler was introduced. He began quietly, giving his version of recent German history. As he proceeded he became angry; so did many of his listeners. Hitler had prepared for this. A group of ex-soldiers armed with truncheons attacked hecklers and threw them out of the hall. Soon the cheering began to drown the interruptions.

Eventually Hitler came to the heart of his speech; the twenty-five-point programme. He asked the audience to give their judgement on each point as he introduced it.

The first point demanded the union of all Germans, including those then living in Austria, Czechoslovakia and Poland, into a Greater Germany. This could probably be achieved only by force. The second point was the abolition of the Treaty of Versailles and the Austrian Peace Treaty of St. Germain. The third point called for colonies to provide food and living space for the surplus population.

Anti-semitism

By the fourth point, Hitler had reached the question of Germany's Jews. Five points were devoted to the Jews. They were to be denied citizenship and the right to hold offices. Any who had entered Germany since August 1914 were to be expelled. The remaining seventeen points dealt mostly with the economy and welfare. They were similar in many ways to the policies of socialist and communist parties in Europe. For example, they called for the state to take over some private businesses and improve social welfare, health and educational opportunities. In addition, Hitler called for newspaper censorship, a 'people's' army and limited religious freedom.

The NSDAP

As Hitler went through his programme in a speech lasting more than two hours, he gradually won over the whole audience. Anyone who objected was thrown out. By the time the meeting ended, the new party was firmly established. At Hitler's insistence it had already been renamed the National Socialist German Workers' Party. In German the full name of the Party was *National Sozialistische Deutsche Arbeiter Partei* (NSDAP), which was soon abbreviated to 'Nazi'.

Party boss

Hitler and Eckhart

The success of the Hofbrauhaus meeting established Hitler as the dominant person in the Nazi Party. He was helped a lot at first by Dietrich Eckhart, a nationalist and a Jew-hater. Eckhart was also a drunkard and a drug-addict but he had been to university and could have been a professor. He smartened up Hitler in speech and dress and introduced him to rich and important people. In March 1920 Eckhart and Hitler flew to Berlin in an open plane when it seemed a revolution was beginning against the Weimar government. By the time they reached Berlin, the 'revolution', known as the Kapp *putsch*, was fizzling out. However, the journey was not entirely wasted. They stayed on in Berlin meeting even more important people including the First World War Chief of the General Staff, General Erich von Lüdendorff.

Völkischer Beobachter

Hitler returned to Munich, was demobbed from the army and rented a small room. This was close to the offices of the *Völkischer Beobachter*, a viciously anti-semitic and anti-communist newspaper. One headline could be translated as 'Do a Real Job on the Jews'. A few months later the Nazis bought the paper which was going bankrupt.

Orator in the making

When he wasn't reading hate stories or sitting in cafes, Hitler was building up the Nazi Party. He did this mainly by his speeches in public two or three times a week. He usually began standing stiffly to attention. Soon he began to relax. He cracked jokes and had question-and-answer sessions both with himself acting two parts, and with people planted in the audience. He learnt to vary the volume and speed of his voice. He made wild gestures with his hands and worked himself up into a state of anger, screaming and spitting. He repeated himself deliberately. He believed people needed to hear a message repeated many times before they remembered it. He cared not whether he was speaking the truth or lies. The bigger the lie, he thought, the more traces it left behind.

As in the Hofbrauhaus in February 1920, Hitler had to put up with angry interruptions. He enjoyed these. Sometimes he replied. Mostly the ex-soldiers around the hall dealt with the hecklers, swiftly and brutally.

Bavarian politics

Less than a year after the Hofbrauhaus meeting the first national congress of the NSDAP was held in Munich. Only 400 delegates arrived. A week later, however, Hitler organised a rally against the war reparations. Thousands turned up. Hitler's speech was received with long cheers. Within a year he had become the most important right-wing politician in Bavaria. The state government, like Hitler, hated the socialists of the Weimar Republic. The original members of the old German Workers' Party were not so happy about Hitler. They did not like the kind of men who were joining the NSDAP; the new members were rough, violent and uneducated. Hitler claimed to be a socialist but, the old members believed, he spent too much time with businessmen and bankers. The 'twenty-five-point programme' called for the abolition of the professional army but they noted that Hitler was friendly with General Lüdendorff and other senior officers.

Leader of the NSDAP

Hitler acted swiftly against the old guard. On 11 July 1921 he offered his resignation from the Party. Then he announced he would not return unless he was chairman and absolute leader. This meant that all members must obey him without question. Without Hitler, the Party would have been nothing. Before the end of the month a special congress of the Nazi Party was called. By a vote of 543 to 1, Hitler was given the position and powers he demanded. That was the last democratic vote ever taken in the Party; henceforth, Hitler made all the decisions.

Street-fighter

It was clear by this time that Hitler's principal aim was to secure power in Germany. Gaining control of the Nazi Party was the first step. The next was to win in the streets. To do this, Hitler needed a private army. These were already commonplace in Germany. For example, the *Freikorps* and the *Stahlhelm* (steel helmet) were, like Hitler's followers, right-wing and mostly ex-soldiers.

The SA

In August 1921 the men who stewarded Hitler's meetings were formed into regular squads. These were called the 'Gymnastic and Sports Division'. Two months later, they were renamed *Sturmabteilung* (storm-troopers) which was abbreviated to SA. They wore brown uniforms and jackboots and so were also known as brownshirts.

Nazi SA (Storm-troopers) parade through Munich

The swastika

The SA had another item of uniform – the swastika armband. Hitler designed the Nazi emblem himself. The swastika, or crooked cross, is an ancient symbol which Hitler placed in a white circle on a red background. Red was also the colour of the communists, so Hitler was perhaps claiming that he too represented the 'masses'. Swastika flags were carried at rallies.

Hitler arrested again

The brownshirted SA bullies, carrying rubber truncheons and whips, became the most feared men in Germany. Soon they were breaking up the meetings of their political opponents. On 14 September 1921 in Munich, SA men savagely beat the principal speaker before he could begin his speech. Hitler was charged by the police and informed he would be put on trial. This didn't put him off. Within two months, Hitler and fifty SA men were involved in a savage fight with several hundred opponents who tried to break up his speech at the Hofbrauhaus in Munich. The SA men fought so ferociously that they cleared the hall. However, Hitler was unable to speak that night.

Hitler was convinced that victory came to the strongest and most ruthless. His battles had given him and the Nazis plenty of publicity. They also brought him a three-month jail sentence but he was released after only one month.

'Battle' of Coburg

Even more publicity came nearly a year later in October 1922. In Italy, Mussolini's black-shirted fascists were gaining strength by marches into towns they said were 'Bolshevik' – where local leaders were trade unionists, socialists or communists. Hitler declared that Coburg, 250 kilometres north of Munich, was a 'bolshevik' town. Accompanied by 600 SA men and a brass band, Hitler headed there in a special train, picking up 200 reinforcements on the way.

On arrival at Coburg, the Nazis marched through the town. They were greeted by angry shouts. As the march continued the citizens began to throw stones. Hitler ordered his men to attack and a short pitched battle followed during which the Nazis drove off their attackers.

Mussolini

The next morning the communists and socialists of Coburg called for 10,000 workers to gather and throw the Nazis out. By that time the number of Nazis had doubled to 1500. They paraded unmolested through the town. Hitler was convinced that his vicious use of force had again brought him victory. So the 'battle' of Coburg became a Nazi honour and a special medal was struck. Two weeks later, Mussolini seemed to prove him right. The blackshirts marched into Rome on 28 October 1922 and Mussolini quickly became dictator of Italy. 'Germany's Mussolini is called Hitler' shouted one of his (Hitler's) men.

One of the storm-troopers later tried to explain his devotion to Hitler:

'It was our feelings that led us to Hitler. What we felt, what our hearts compelled us to think, was this – Hitler, you're our man. You talk like a human being who's been at the front, who's been through the same mess we were in, and not in some soft berth, but like us as an unknown soldier. You are pleading, with all your being, with all your burning heart, for us, the Germans.'

Autobiography of Obersturmführer Georg Zeidler, 1934.

Hitler's men

Ernst Röhm

Captain Ernst Röhm was Hitler's most important assistant in the first years of the party. He commanded the SA. Not only was the burly Röhm a ruthless fighter on the streets, he was also a skilful political organiser, having acted as link-man between the *Freikorps* and the army in 1919. He helped to raise the money to buy the *Völkischer Beobachter* and he established the SA as the efficient force of the Nazi Party. Röhm recognised Hitler's skills as a speaker and supported him strongly but never saw Hitler as a friend.

Julius Streicher

Julius Streicher was another violent man who joined the party in 1922. He brought with him followers from his 'German Socialist Party'. Streicher hated the Jews, and in particular, the idea of non-Jewish Germans and Jews marrying. He had his own weekly paper *The Stormer* which was full of vicious obscene stories and cartoons attacking the Jews.

Rudolf Hess

Rudolf Hess had been born in Egypt. He served in the First World War as a soldier and then a pilot. He studied history and economics at Munich University, joining the Nazi Party in 1920. Unlike Röhm and Streicher, Hess was not personally a violent man and not regarded as a leader although he became Hitler's deputy.

Hermann Göring

Hermann Göring had also been a fighter pilot in the First World War and a public hero after shooting down twenty-two enemy aircraft. By 1918 he was in command of the Richthöfen ('Red Baron') Squadron. The Treaty of Versailles ended his chance of an air-force career so Göring became a private pilot. He married a wealthy Swedish divorcée and settled in Munich. He joined the Nazis in 1923 after listening to a Hitler speech and was given command of the Munich SA. Göring was a highly intelligent man, an anti-communist but not as obsessed with the Jews as Hitler and Streicher.

Alfred Rosenberg

Alfred Rosenberg was the Nazi Party's 'intellectual'. He was born in Estonia, then part of the Russian empire, and educated at Moscow University. After the Russian revolution Rosenberg emigrated to Germany. He made his way to Munich and met Dietrich Eckart. Both hated the Jews and wrote anti-semitic pamphlets. Rosenberg joined the German Workers' Party and became the Party's 'expert' on the USSR and the new states which lay between the USSR and Germany. He and Hitler spent a lot of time in cafes discussing politics.

These men were typical of the thousands of Germans who were supporting Hitler by 1923. Like Hitler most had good war records although younger hooligan groups were also wearing the SA brownshirts by this time. They were fiercely nationalist, anti-communist and anti-semitic. They felt that Germany had been betrayed by the politicians of the Weimar Republic and humiliated by the Versailles Treaty. Their own careers had been destroyed and they had suffered hunger and poverty. By 1923 millions of Germans were facing poverty from a new threat – massive inflation.

The great inflation

Economic troubles

By 1920 Germany's economy was in a desperate condition. During the war, the German government had raised huge loans of 144 billion marks (equal to well over £250 billion at 1990 prices). These loans plus interest would have to be repaid out of future taxation. Between 1914 and 1919 the German mark had lost more than half its value against the dollar. Although this made imports more expensive and exports cheaper, Germany had lost many overseas markets during the war and could not sell enough abroad to buy the food and other things needed. The important industrial areas such as the Saarland, Lorraine and Silesia had been lost. With the threat of a communist revolution few people were willing to invest money in new industries. Finally, in 1921, Germany was ordered to pay the huge sum in reparations, payable over forty-two years, plus a quarter of all its exports.

Thus the German government owed huge sums to both its own citizens and to the Allies. Factories could not produce or sell enough goods to pay for imports and food shortages continued. Nobody had any confidence in the country or its currency.

The Ruhr

The result was that by 1921 the mark began to lose value rapidly. Germany fell behind in reparations payments. In January 1922 the new French government took a hard line, saying Germany could but would not pay. Germany missed further payments. The British and French argued about what to do and finally the French lost patience. On 11 January 1923 French and Belgian troops marched into the Ruhr, the great coal- and steel-producing area of Germany.

The French believed their action would make the Germans restart payments. The result was the opposite. Germany's political leaders made outraged speeches and the Ruhr workers went on strike with the government's backing. Extremists moved into the Ruhr, committing terrorist acts to stop the coal being moved out. One saboteur was captured by the French, tried and executed, and became a national hero. Other German workers were killed fighting French troops. The French brought in their own workers to run the Ruhr industries. This was intended to make sure the reparations were paid and that Germany would remain weak and poor. Most Germans were already becoming poor as the mark fell in value at increasing speed.

The falling mark

This shows how many marks bought 1 US dollar's worth of goods:

1914	4
1919	9
1921 (Nov.)	70
1922 (Jan.)	192
1922 (Aug.)	1000
1923 (Jan.)	18,000
1923 (July)	160,000
1923 (Aug.)	1,000,000
1923 (Nov.)	4.2 billion

Paper money became totally worthless. One story tells of a man who left a wheelbarrow full of banknotes. When he returned the banknotes were in the gutter and the wheelbarrow had been stolen! People preferred to exchange their goods for other goods rather than for money. Workers were paid twice daily and spent their wages immediately before they lost more value.

As the mark fell in value, ever larger amounts were needed. By late 1923 the government had 300 papermills and 2000 printing works on twenty-four hour shifts to provide the paper currency.

Winners and losers

The government deliberately encouraged the inflation. It was able to pay off the First World War debt with useless paper. Germany's great industrialists also paid off their debts. Others borrowed money and used it to buy up companies, even business empires. A few weeks later they repaid the debt with cash which was of little value. Foreigners with dollars, pounds and francs could buy anything they fancied.

Most ordinary Germans lost heavily. In 1923 a man had to work for twenty-two hours to buy a kilo of margarine and for six weeks to buy a pair of boots. Savings accounts were destroyed in a few days. Old people on fixed pensions faced starvation.

Rallies in Bavaria

Hitler stayed well away from the Ruhr in early 1923. He refused to co-operate with other political parties but in any case had been banned from speaking in most of Germany. Instead he organised a series of Nazi rallies in Bavaria against the German government. The police tried to ban these rallies but Hitler went ahead. The next day a huge rally of 6000 SA men was held in bitter weather at the Marsfeld in Munich. There was no disorder and Hitler's reputation increased.

In April he made speeches attacking the Weimar politicians, the French and the Jews. On May Day he defied the Bavarian government and held another big rally of armed SA in Munich. He hoped to provoke the Communists to attack him; then he would seize power. Instead the SA men were disarmed by police and troops.

The beer hall *putsch*

It seemed that Hitler was missing his opportunities. He had not taken part in the struggle against the French in the Ruhr and could not even defy his own government in Bavaria. Hitler was not worried. He went on holiday whilst the political and economic crisis in Germany got worse. 4000 people were joining the Nazi Party each month.

Gustav Stresemann

On 12 August 1923 a new national government – the seventh since 1919 – took office in Germany. The Chancellor was Gustav Stresemann, one of the few outstanding politicians of this period. His government was made up of a coalition of moderate parties together with his own Centre Party. Six weeks later, realising that Germany was facing total economic collapse, he ordered the end of resistance to the French and the resumption of reparations payments.

Bavaria opposes Weimar

The Nazis and the Communists attacked this decision. Each believed they could seize power if the crisis lasted long enough. Bavaria seemed the most likely place for Nazi success. Its politicians were bitterly hostile to the democratic government in Weimar. They gave three men, a politician Gustav von Kahr, a General, Otto von Lossow, and the police chief Hans von Seisser, full powers to oppose the Weimar Government. Yet to overthrow Stresemann would mean that the Bavarians would have to declare themselves independent from the rest of Germany or lead a 'march on Berlin'.

Stresemann's reply

Stresemann realised the serious danger of civil war and looked for a way of convincing the Bavarians that he was a patriotic German. He did this by attacking the socialist/communist governments of Saxony and Thuringia. The Weimar army marched in and overthrew these state governments.

The Bavarians were impressed. Hitler was worried because without the support of Bavarian leaders he had little chance of seizing power. He decided he must get the army and police in Bavaria to support him and make his bid for power.

Meeting in the beer hall

On 6 November a brief notice appeared in a Munich paper. It stated that von Kahr was to address a meeting at the Bürgerbraukeller, a huge beer hall in Munich. Hitler refused an official invitation to attend. Instead he saw it as an opportunity to seize von Kahr, von Lossow and von Seisser who would also be there. Hitler would then declare his revolution against the Weimar government and force the three men to join him in direct action to bring down Stresemann's government.

The meeting began quietly at 8.30 p.m. Von Kahr began a long, boring speech. Hitler, his bodyguard Ulrich Graf and two other Nazis stood listening in the hall. They were all drinking beer at a billion marks a glass! Suddenly the doors burst open and in marched Hermann Göring and his stormtroopers. Hitler fired a pistol shot into the ceiling and leapt on to the platform.

The *putsch*

'The National Revolution has begun' he shouted. 'There are 600 heavily armed men around the hall. The Bavarian and Reich (national)

Hitler greets men who took part in the putsch

governments have been removed and a provisional national government formed. The army and police are marching on the city under the swastika banner.'

This was the beer-hall *putsch* (seizure of power). It was all a big lie. Hitler hoped the Bavarian leaders would believe it and join him. By this time General Lüdendorff had arrived, summoned by Hitler to 'lead' the revolution. Lüdendorff, one of the ruling generals of the First World War, was still a powerful presence. Overawed by his arrival and threatened by Hitler's pistol, von Kahr and the others agreed to support him. Hitler then announced their agreement and the formation of a new national government. Meanwhile Röhm, accompanied by several hundred SA men and soldiers, seized the local military headquarters.

Hitler left the beer hall later and General von Lossow, quickly followed by von Seisser and von Kahr, made an excuse and escaped into the night. Von Lossow began telephoning army units outside the city to come to Munich and crush the uprising. Von Kahr announced that the Nazi Party had been dissolved.

**The government
stands firm**

By next morning Hitler had 4000 men in the city. But it was clear that the Weimar government had not been overthrown. Moreover army units were already in Munich and had Captain Röhm and his 150 men trapped in the military headquarters. At Lüdendorff's suggestion, Hitler decided to try a desperate gamble. He lined up his men for a march on the headquarters to rescue Röhm. Lüdendorff was convinced the troops and police would obey him. Shortly before noon 3000 armed men, led by the ex-general and the ex-corporal, left the beer hall and headed for the city centre. The first police cordon on the Ludwig Bridge was overrun. The second cordon of 100 city police, armed with rifles, was blocking a narrow street leading into the Odeonsplatz, a broad square. Ulrich Graf, Hitler's bodyguard, ran ahead shouting, 'Don't shoot, Lüdendorff and Hitler are coming!' Then as Hitler shouted 'surrender!' the shooting began. The man with whom Hitler was marching was mortally wounded. He fell, dragging Hitler down and dislocating his shoulder. Three policemen and sixteen marchers lay dead. Only Lüdendorff kept marching, through the cordon and into the square where he was arrested.

Arrested again

Hitler was bundled into a car and driven to a house in the country. Göring was wounded and after treatment by a Jewish doctor fled to Austria. Hess also escaped to Austria but Röhm surrendered and was arrested. Two days later Hitler was arrested and charged with treason.

Mein Kampf

Hitler on trial

The trial began on 26 February 1924. It lasted twenty-four days and received full coverage in German and foreign newspapers. By this time Hitler had thrown off the depression which he suffered after his failure. He had recovered his self-confidence and took full advantage of the publicity which the trial gave him.

In his defence he said he was acting with the Bavarian government until the very last moment. He also attacked the Weimar governments as the real traitors to Germany. Nevertheless Hitler took full responsibility for the unsuccessful *putsch*. By the end of the trial he was known throughout Germany. Although Lüdendorff was acquitted, Hitler was found guilty. He faced the possibility of a life sentence; he received five years. Clearly he was not regarded as a real traitor in Bavaria.

**Prisoner in
Landsberg**

Hitler served his sentence – or at least nine months of it before he was released – in the fortress of Landsberg, 30 kilometres from Munich. Forty of his followers, including Rudolf Hess who had returned from Austria and been tried, were imprisoned with him. Hitler had more freedom than in a normal criminal prison. The cell doors were unlocked at 6 a.m., breakfast was at 7 a.m. and the prisoners exercised from 8–10 a.m. Hitler took no part in this because of his injured shoulder which was still troubling him six months later. Mail was distributed at noon, followed by lunch. Even in prison Hitler's followers stood to attention to await his entry. In the afternoon, Hitler read or wrote letters in his cell. He walked in the fortress garden for an hour after tea. Supper was at 6 p.m. followed by more recreation. Lights-out was at 10 p.m. Hitler had as many visitors as he wished, usually in his cell.

'My struggle'

During the last five months of his imprisonment, Hitler worked on his autobiography. The book was the idea of Max Amann, Hitler's business manager, to pay the legal costs of the trial. Amann also changed the title. Hitler wanted to call it 'Four-and-a-half years of struggle against lies, stupidity, and cowardice'. Amann suggested *Mein Kampf* – 'My Struggle'. If Hitler was a forceful speaker, he was certainly no great writer. The text which appeared was hundreds of pages of heavy, dull and long-winded prose explaining Hitler's ideas. It had to be published as two volumes. It was not the kind of thing Max Amann had hoped for. The first print run of 10,000 sold out but by 1930 sales had reached only 23,000. Foreign-language translations did not appear for many years – in Britain and the USA in 1939.

Release

On 18 September 1924, only six months after the beginning of Hitler's five-year sentence, the Governor at Landsberg sent a report to the Bavarian Ministry of Justice. He praised Hitler as a man of 'strict discipline and order, co-operative, modest and courteous', especially to the warders. It would be quite safe to release Hitler. He would not be violent again. The Bavarian State Police opposed early release but he was freed on 19 December.

This was part of Hitler's first speech to the Nazi faithful after his release from prison:

'My task as leader of the movement is not to look for the causes of a previous quarrel or to assess who was right, but to mould the movement into a unified weapon regardless of the interests of individuals. Thus I shall not inquire into the past of those comrades who rejoin, but only work to ensure that the past will not repeat itself in the future. From our supporters I demand that if they are willing to join the new movement they should feel themselves once more to be brothers in a great fighting community and stand together loyally shoulder to shoulder as before.

But I expect the leaders, in so far as they come from the old camp, to give me the same obedience as we all give to the common idea.

Those who cannot forget the past are not worthy of serving a better future.

I myself promise to render an account to the comrades in a year's time as to whether the Party has become a movement or whether the movement has suffocated by being a party.

In either case I shall take the responsibility.

Long live the National Socialist German Workers' Party!

Long live our German fatherland!'

4
Rebuilding the Nazi Party 1924–1929

Nazism in check?

A split party

Although out of prison, Hitler was on parole. Any misbehaviour and he could have been brought back to serve the full sentence. A second problem was that he was stateless between 1925 and 1932. Austria removed his citizenship and Germany refused to grant him papers and a passport. A third problem was that until 1927 he was banned from making public speeches in most parts of Germany.

As well as these problems, Hitler was faced with an internal split in the Nazi Party. Some party members led by Gregor Strasser and Rosenberg had joined with Lüdendorff to form the National Socialist Freedom Movement. This grouping came second in the Bavarian State Elections in April 1924 and got 2 million votes and thirty-two seats in the national election the following month. Hitler was opposed totally to seeing the Nazis swallowed up in a larger grouping. However, those favouring a merger were more numerous.

Regaining control

After his release, Hitler set about trying to regain complete control of the Party. He persuaded the Bavarian government to lift its ban on his making public speeches. His first speech was so successful and created such a storm that the ban was quickly reimposed. More immediately serious was the challenge from Strasser who was building up the Nazi Party in northern Germany and developing socialist policies which Hitler could not support. Most members lived in southern Germany where Hitler had control. In February 1926 the northerners and southerners met at Bamberg. The southerners were in the majority and Hitler completely dominated the meeting, speaking for five hours. The northerners agreed to follow Hitler. At a general meeting three months later Hitler was confirmed as supreme *Führer* (leader).

Dr Goebbels

One member who had not been won over at Bamberg but was soon to be an ardent follower was Joseph Goebbels. Born in the Rhineland in 1897, Goebbels suffered poliomyelitis at the age of four. His right leg became permanently twisted and shortened. He grew to be only 5 feet (1.5 metres) tall. He had to wear a surgical boot and was rejected at once in 1914 when he tried to join the army. Instead of fighting he had a brilliant university career, gaining his Doctorate in Philosophy in 1921. He first met Hitler in 1925. Hitler recognised his talents, particularly as a speaker, and set out to win his support. By the middle of 1926 Goebbels was devoted to Hitler, who repaid his loyalty by making him party manager in Berlin. Goebbels made the Nazis a powerful force in the city although not as strong as the socialists or communists.

The SS

Whilst Hitler had regained complete control of the Nazi Party by mid-1926, he was unhappy about the SA. The storm-troopers were always ready to have a street-fight or throw hecklers out of meetings. However, many of them did not like taking orders from 'civilians'. Hitler was not sure he would be able to trust them always. In 1925 he established a special protection squad or *Schutzstaffel* (SS) as his bodyguard. The SS wore the same uniform as the SA with a black cap and tie. They were Hitler's bodyguard and regarded themselves as 'special'. In January 1929 Hitler appointed Heinrich Himmler to command the SS.

Rallies at Nuremburg

Since Hitler was the supreme leader of the Nazi Party, there was no need for an annual meeting to decide policies. Hitler decided them. Instead, the party held dramatic rallies to encourage loyalty and to win publicity. Hitler chose the city of Nuremburg for these rallies. The first

The huge Nuremburg Rallies went on until the early 1940s

was in 1927. 30,000 Nazis, mostly SA men, arrived in nearly 50 special trains. The Nuremburg rallies consisted of a march past Hitler and the leaders. Then there would be a long speech from Hitler about how the party had begun and what it was going to do. Each year the numbers at the rally grew larger and the event more spectacular.

Election failures

Despite Hitler's efforts the NSDAP remained a small party. In 1926 it had perhaps 35,000 members. At the national election in December 1924 the party had gained less than 1 million votes out of more than 33 million. The number of Nazi deputies fell to fourteen. In May 1928 at the next election only twelve Nazis were elected out of the thirty-six who had stood for one of the 489 seats. Meanwhile, following the death of President Ebert, Field Marshal Paul von Hindenburg had been elected President of the Republic on 26 February 1925. With the return of prosperity the German voters had turned to an old soldier, who had commanded their armies in the First World War.

The revival of Germany

Better times

Hitler had built up the NSDAP during the crisis years of 1920–23. During periods of hunger and inflation people listened to extremist ideas, like Hitler's. From 1924 the situation in Germany changed for the better. In prison Hitler decided that he would seek power only through elections. Clearly, after 1924 only a very small percentage of Germans thought the Nazis worth voting for.

The situation in Germany got much better for two reasons. First the economy improved. Second Germany had much better relationships with its former enemies. The economy began to improve after Stresemann agreed to restart reparations in 1923. At the same time he began to cure the great inflation. A new currency, the rentenmark, was issued. Only 2.4 billion marks were circulated in notes. Government spending was cut back. 300,000 government officials and workers lost their jobs but people now had confidence that the economy was under control and they could trust the currency. The inflation ended.

Charles Dawes' plan

The former Western Allies realised that the system of reparations payments would have to be changed. A weak Germany could not pay; only a strong German economy could afford it. So it was important to help Germany to recover and to stop treating the Germans as outcasts. A new scheme for reparations was drawn up by the American General Charles Dawes in 1924. Germany would pay a much lower figure which would vary between £50 million and £125 million according to the country's prosperity in each year.

Stresemann's policies

Gustav Stresemann, now the German Foreign Minister, was pleased by the changing attitudes of Britain, France and the USA. Like most Germans, he hated the Treaty of Versailles and wanted to get back the lost territories. But he had no wish to see Germany fighting another war and so applied to join the League of Nations.

Stresemann's policies were very successful. Germany was admitted to the League in 1926 but before that two important treaties were signed. In 1925 Belgium, France and Germany signed the Locarno Pact promising never to fight a war to change their frontiers. Britain and Italy also signed the Pact, promising to take action against any country which broke it. The following year Germany and the USSR signed the Treaty of Berlin to prevent a war between the two countries. Germany also wanted to prevent an alliance between France and Russia. The high point in the search for peace was reached in 1928 with the signing of the Kellogg-Briand Pact. Sixty-five nations, including Germany, promised never to launch an aggressive war.

Owen Young's plan

Stresemann gained one more success before his death on 8 October 1929. The Allies agreed to withdraw their soldiers from the Rhineland. In return the final settlement of the reparations question would be made. Under the chairmanship of Owen Young, a committee met in Paris early in 1929. The Young Plan reduced Germany's total bill from 132 billion marks to 37 billion. Payments were to be made until 1988.

Germany prospers

By late 1929 German industry was in much better condition than in 1913 and exports were up by one-third in value. One reason for this success was American investment. About 25 billion marks flowed into Germany from the USA up to 1929. This money was used for two purposes. The first was the modernisation of factories, steelworks and coal mines. The second was improvement of such things as roads, railways, canals, docks, electric power stations and housing. By 1929 the horrors of 1919–23 were being forgotten. Wages and living standards were rising. The 1928 election reflected a feeling that there was no need to vote for extremist parties such as the Nazis and the Communists.

This was Konrad Heiden's memory of Germany in 1925:

Again there was work for all; there was money for those who knew how to make it; there was enough food; for those with the sweet tooth there was whipped cream – a sign of prosperity that appeared very late in the German post-war world. Again there were silk stockings and even pure silk dresses; women began to use lipstick; the first radios croaked; even people who were not immeasurably wealthy began to buy automobiles; more people began to travel in the little airplanes permitted by the Versailles Treaty – and negotiations for larger ones were proceeding in Paris. Passport regulations, travel restrictions, closed borders vanished . . . American financiers went to Germany looking for factories willing to borrow good American dollars from them. German scholars again appeared at foreign scientific congresses. French students went to Germany and invited their German comrades to youth congresses and festivals at Paris or Geneva. A Zeppelin flew from Germany to America; a German car won the first prize at a big automobile race in Italy; a German of Jewish descent won the world chess championship.'

Konrad Heiden, *Der Führer*, Book One, 1944.

Re-organising the NSDAP

Hitler prospers

Despite the failure of the NSDAP to get wide support in the elections of 1924 and 1928, Hitler regarded this period as one of the happiest of his life. One reason was that he was quite well off. The publication of the two volumes of *Mein Kampf* in 1926 and 1927 brought him a steady flow of money. So did a series of newspaper articles for which he was paid large fees. In 1927 he was able to rent cheaply a house at Berchtesgaden in the Alps. This quickly became his favourite home.

Hitler could also feel happy about his revival of the NSDAP; he had acquired full control again. Membership was growing, although not as quickly as Hitler would have liked. Early in 1927 the ban on Hitler's making speeches was lifted.

The gauleiters

Meanwhile, in preparation for the day when he would have complete power, he divided the country into thirty-four districts or *Gaus*, each under the command of a *Gauleiter*. *Gaus* were sub-divided into *Kreis*. Within each *Kreis* were several *Ortsgruppen*, each the size of a city. Within each *Ortsgruppe* there were further sub-divisions to cover each street or housing complex. Hitler also appointed a 'shadow cabinet' so he would be ready to take over the government. The NSDAP owned three newspapers which ran vicious attacks on the Weimar governments.

If Hitler personally had enough money, the Party didn't. It was an expensive business to operate a political party. In the late 1920s there was no reason for any wealthy people to offer big money to the NSDAP.

The bachelor Führer

In April 1929 Hitler celebrated his 40th birthday. He was still unmarried. After 1919 as he was building up the Nazi Party, Hitler decided to stay single because as an unmarried man he would appear more attractive to women voters. Women were given the vote in several countries, including Germany, after the First World War. Women were also in the majority in the adult population because of male emigration before the war and the losses of soldiers from 1914–18.

There is no doubt that Hitler was very attractive to women. Equally, he thoroughly enjoyed the company of women, especially young and pretty ones. He was not a homosexual nor did he suffer from syphilis as some enemies claimed. He was deeply attached to his half-niece Geli Raubal and during his last fourteen years to Eva Braun.

Collapse on Wall Street

In October 1929 an event important to Germany occurred. This was the collapse of the Wall Street Stock Exchange in New York. During the 1920s vast sums of money had been spent buying shares and land in America. This had sent up prices rapidly and the shares were priced far beyond their real value. The bubble burst and share prices fell by $40 billion in the first month. American banks began demanding repayments of the money they had lent to German industry. In their turn German firms were forced to cut production. Unemployment rose rapidly and Germany's prosperity was at an end.

Hitler's opportunity was coming.

5

The Road to Power, 1929–33

The Great Depression

At the end of 1929 Hitler may not have realised that his political fortunes were about to improve dramatically. Yet he was involved in two issues which would lift him into the forefront of German politics. The first was the campaign against the Young Plan for re-organising reparations. The Plan pleased some Germans because it eased the country's economic difficulties but it angered nationalists. They claimed that willingness to pay even smaller reparations meant that Germany was admitting her 'war guilt'.

Hitler and Hugenburg

One man who strongly refused to accept this guilt was Alfred Hugenburg. He was head of the Germany National Party as well as owner of a chain of cinemas and newspapers. Hugenburg and Hitler joined forces temporarily to fight the Young Plan. Hitler became famous throughout Germany as he blamed the Plan for the way that German's economy had suddenly begun to turn for the worse. People began to send money to the Nazi's treasury. There was never enough for all the Party's needs but it did pay for a smart new Nazi headquarters, the Brown House, in Munich. It opened in late 1930.

Unemployment
CAUSED BY WALL ST. CRASH.

The true reason for the downturn in the economy was the second reason for Hitler's improved position. This was the world economic depression which followed the New York stock market crash. As world *WALL STREET CRASH 1929.* prices for agricultural products fell, German farmers were affected and many went bankrupt. Although the government did provide some financial help for them, it was not enough. Many farmers began to listen to Hitler's propaganda which promised them greater help. Heavy industry was also badly affected. The export of ships, machinery, steel, electrical and chemical goods collapsed.

Between 1928 and 1932 German exports fell by 55 per cent, near to the world average fall in trade of 62 per cent. Unemployment rose rapidly. It was less than 1 million in 1929; it reached 3 million by mid 1930, 5 million by the spring of 1931 and 6 million by early 1932.

'I am looking for work of any kind'

These were the official figures. The true figures, counting those who didn't get unemployment benefit, were much higher.

Government by decree, 1930

Müller

After the 1928 election, Germany was ruled by a Socialist-Centrist coalition government under Hermann Müller. In March 1930 this coalition broke up after the Socialists objected to cuts in unemployment benefits. President Hindenburg disliked the Weimar system of government by parliamentary democracy. In particular he disliked the Socialists. He did not therefore support Müller, who resigned.

Brüning

In his place, Hindenburg appointed the Centre Party leader Heinrich Brüning (1885–1970) as Chancellor. From this time on the Weimar Republic ceased to be a parliamentary democracy. With the Socialists opposed to him, Brüning had no majority in the Reichstag. He ruled by Presidential Decree, using powers that Chancellors had under Articles 48 and 53 of the Weimar Constitution.

Presidential Decree meant that Hindenburg alone could decide to declare a 'state of emergency'. He decided what steps should be taken to deal with it and ordered them to be carried out in his decrees which had the force of law. The Reichstag had the power to overturn them only if asked to vote on them. This happened to Brüning on 18 July 1930. The Reichstag was dissolved and by law a new election had to be held within sixty days. This was fixed for 14 September.

Hitler campaigning

Hitler began a vigorous election campaign of marches, rallies and speeches. His posters screamed out promises and made violent attacks upon the 'enemies' of the country. At the major rallies, the Nazis used every trick they could to win support. In one of the new stadiums, 100,000 people would be gathered awaiting the arrival of the Party leader. Suddenly, they would all lean forward and the word passed 'Hitler is coming . . . Hitler is here – Heil Hitler!' A fanfare of trumpets would sound and the cheering begin. Hitler, dressed in his storm-trooper's uniform, would march smartly out into the centre of the arena, his arm held aloft in the Nazi salute.

Then the speech would begin. For two hours or more Hitler would promise and plead, rant and rave, curse and cajole. His words echoed like a whiplash around the cheering thousands. When at last he had finished, he would climb into his huge black open Mercedes-Benz. Then once again giving the outstretched arm salute, he would be carried out of the stadium amidst a final roar of cheers.

As the car left, a torchlight procession of several hundred SS men would march in whilst fireworks broke overhead. Then massed bands struck up and the whole assembly joined in the singing of '*Deutschland Über Alles*'[1] and (in later years) the 'Horst Wessel Song'[2].

The SA

These openly violent and spectacular methods of the Nazis drew many supporters. Ex-soldiers were attracted by the uniforms and banners. Many Germans were impressed by what seemed to be the irresistible force of the SA. Supporters of the other parties probably watched the Nazi show of force and realised that if 'you can't beat 'em, join 'em'. Many others who were repelled by Nazism must have been frightened into silence by Nazi brutalities. Hitler at first believed that the SA was his trump card. He went out of his way to encourage their activities, and glorify those members who were killed or wounded.

By 1930 the SA was probably about 100,000 strong. The majority were unemployed young men. They were once more under the command of Captain Ernst Röhm. He had spent the previous five years in South America training the Bolivian Army. The SA steadily won the street battles for Hitler but it was too socialist for his liking. It was also becoming too independent, sometimes refusing to march. Thus Hitler began to favour his bodyguard, the SS.

Himmler and the SS

When Heinrich Himmler took command of the SS in January 1929 it had only 280 members. He had been a member of the SA since 1923. He had marched through Munich that year with Hitler and Lüdendorff

---

[1] 'Germany above all others'

[2] Horst Wessel was a young SA man killed during a street fight with the Communists in 1931. He rapidly became a Nazi martyr.

when they tried to seize power. Since then Himmler had become well known for his keenness and loyalty. However, Himmler was a strange fellow with an interest in astrology and spiritualism. He also believed in reincarnation. In his former life, Himmler believed, he had been Henry the Fowler, a medieval German king!

As soon as he took over, Himmler began recruiting more men into the SS. By December 1929 it was 1000 strong. A year later it had over 2700 men. Then Hitler announced that the SS was to be independent of the SA. To show its independence, the SS began to wear a new uniform, totally black.

The Prussian Ministry of the Interior had agents watching the NSDAP. In May 1930 they reported:

'The Reichstag and Landtag deputies of the Party and many other Party speakers travel about every day to undertake and build up this agitation. Through systematic training courses, through correspondence courses, and recently through a school for NSDAP speakers established on 1 July 1929, such agitators are trained for this task over a period of months, even years. If they prove themselves, they receive official recognition from the Party and are put under contract to give at least thirty speeches over a period of eight months and receive as an incentive a fee of 20 Reichsmarks or more per evening in addition to their expenses. Rhetorical skill combined with subjects carefully chosen to suit the particular audience, which in the countryside and in the small towns is mainly interested in economic matters, ensure, according to our observations, halls which are almost invariably overcrowded with enthusiastic listeners. Meetings with an audience of between 1000 and 5000 people are a daily occurrence in the bigger towns. Frequently a second or several parallel meetings have to be held because the halls provided cannot hold the numbers who attend . . . On such occasions the network of local branches is extended as far as possible or at all events contact men are recruited who are intended to prepare the ground through intensive propaganda by word of mouth for the spread of the movement which can be observed everywhere. Frequently such propaganda squads stay in a certain place for several days and try to win the local population for the movement through the most varied sorts of entertainment such as concerts, sports days, tattoos in suitable places, and even church parades.'

The Nazi break-through, 1930–32   GLEICHALTUNG

Second largest party

The results of the 1930 election amazed even Hitler. The NSDAP gained over 6 million votes. This was 18 per cent of the total. It won 107 seats and became the second largest party after the Socialists (143 seats). The Communists, with 77 seats, also made big gains. But the Centre Party won only 68 and Hugenburg's Nationalists dropped to 41 seats. 40 per cent of Germans had voted for the Nazis, the Communists or another extremist party. All were opposed to the Weimar Republic and government based on laws passed in the Reichstag.

The principal reason for Hitler's massive gains was the economic collapse and the rapidly rising unemployment. 4 million new young voters took part in their first election. They were unemployed or soon would be after finishing their education. They listened to Hitler's messages and believed in them. The worse the situation became in Germany, the greater the support Hitler could expect.

Increasing depression

For the time being the election results meant that Brüning could continue as Chancellor so long as the Socialists agreed to support him in a coalition. The election itself had made Germany's situation worse. Foreign investors feared the break-up of the state and withdrew over $300 million (equal to $7 billion in 1990) from Germany in the two months after the election. This cost tens of thousands of jobs. Brüning was forced to make more cuts in spending and to raise taxes. This in turn lost more jobs. He was able to make these cuts only because he told the Socialists, 'If you don't support me, the Nazis will take power'. Brüning also said Germany could no longer pay even the reduced reparations of the Young Plan. An international conference to discuss this was delayed until June 1932. It then agreed to end all war payments but by then it was too late to save the Weimar Republic.

Street violence

Within the Reichstag, parliamentary democracy was being destroyed. The newly-elected Nazi deputies wore their brown-shirts and jackboots. They continually interrupted the proceedings with shouts, songs and jokes. Sometimes fights broke out amongst the deputies.

By 1931 there were wars of fists, boots, sticks, knives and even guns on the streets. The SA had recruited thousands of more members in the months following the September 1930 election. The Socialists and trade unions had their *Reichsbanner* and the Communists the *Rotfrontkampferbund* ('Red Front Fighters'). Vicious battles which led to many deaths and even more injuries were fought in the streets and beer-halls of Berlin, Hamburg and other towns and cities. Under the cover of this disorder, savage attacks were made by the SA on Jewish people and property. The worst was in September 1931 in Berlin's most fashionable street, the Kurfurstendamm. Fifty SA men were arrested.

Hitler in the news

Hitler meanwhile had become famous not only in Germany; he was also attracting attention abroad. In Britain there were articles about him in the *Times*, the *Observer*, the *Daily Telegraph* and the *Sunday Express*. Many US papers including the *New York Times*, wrote about him. Germans could not only read about Hitler and the NSDAP, sometimes they could see him in the convoy of open Mercedes cars, with SS guards, which criss-crossed Germany at high speed. Hitler never drove but sat in the front wearing a leather coat, helmet and goggles. He read the maps and ordered last minute route-changes for fear of Communist ambushes. The purpose of these journeys was to make speeches and seek more support at local elections.

Dusseldorf speech

The most important speech Hitler made was at the Industry Club in Dusseldorf on 27 January 1932. He spoke for more than two hours to the leaders of German industry. They were a difficult group to impress. Hitler's violent reputation had gone before him, but by the end of the speech the audience was cheering him wildly. He set out to convince his audience that he was a serious politician; he said he would look after big business if elected and so concentrated his attack on the Communists. He told the industrialists that only the NSDAP could stop the Communists from seizing power; if the Communists succeeded they would seize all big businesses and banks, therefore the industrialists should give money to the NSDAP. Some did, but not enough to solve the Nazis' financial problems.

This is part of Hitler's speech to the Dusseldorf Industry Club:

'I know quite well, gentlemen, that when National Socialists march through the streets and suddenly in the evening there arises a tumult and a commotion, then the bourgeois draws back the window-curtain, looks out, and says: 'Once again my night's rest is disturbed: no more sleep for me. Why must these Nazis always be so provocative and run about the place at night?' Gentlemen, if everyone thought like that, then, true enough, no one's sleep at night would be disturbed, but then also the bourgeois today would not be able to venture into the street. If everyone thought in that way, if these young folk had no ideal to move them and drive them forward, then certainly they would gladly be rid of these nightly fights. But remember that it means sacrifice when today many hundreds of thousands of SA and SS men of the National Socialist movement have every day to mount on their lorries, attend protest meetings, undertake marches, sacrifice themselves night after night and then come back in the grey dawn to workshop and factory, or as unemployed to take the pittance of the dole: it means sacrifice when from the little they possess they have further to buy uniforms, their shirts, their badges, yes and even pay their own fares. Believe me, there is already in all this the force of an ideal – a great ideal! And if the whole German nation today had the same faith in its vocation as these hundreds of thousands, if the whole nation possessed this idealism, Germany would stand in the eyes of the world otherwise than she stands now!' (loud applause)

Hitler for President

Hitler defeated

In the Spring of 1932 Hindenburg's seven-year term of office as President came to an end. At the age of 85 Hindenburg was declining mentally and physically. He wished to retire but was persuaded by Brüning the Chancellor and others to stand for re-election. Hitler offered to support Hindenburg if the latter would make him Chancellor. Hindenburg refused and Hitler decided to stand for President also. First he had to become a German citizen. Eventually it took two ballots before Hindenburg won a 53 per cent majority with 19.4 million votes. Hitler got 13.4 million and Ernst Thälmann, the Communist candidate, 3.7 million. Most moderate Germans had probably voted for Hindenburg. Nevertheless, Hitler's position was greatly strengthened. He was by then one of the most important politicians in Germany.

The Nazi newspaper *Völkischer Beobachter* printed the following on its front page of 3 March 1932, supporting Hitler's candidacy for President:

'. . . The National Socialist Movement, assembled at this hour as a fighting squad around its leader, today calls on the entire German people to join its ranks, and to pave a path that will bring Adolf Hitler to the head of the nation, and thus:

LEAD GERMANY TO FREEDOM

HITLER   is the password of all who believe in Germany's resurrection.

HITLER   is the last hope of those who were deprived of everything: of farm and home, of savings, employment, survival; and who have but one possession left: their faith in a just Germany which will once again grant to its citizens honour, freedom, and bread.

HITLER   is the word of deliverance for millions, for they are in despair, and see only in this name a path to new life and creativity.

HITLER   was bequeathed the legacy of the two million dead comrades of the World War, who died not for the present system of the gradual destruction of our nation, but for Germany's future.

HITLER   is the man of the people hated by the enemy because he understands the people and fights for the people.

HITLER   is the furious will of Germany's youth, which, in the midst of a tired generation, is fighting for new forms, and neither can nor will abandon its faith in a better German future. Hence Hitler is the password and the flaming signal of all who wish for a German future.

All of them, on March 13, will call out to the men of the old system who promised them freedom and dignity, and delivered stones and words instead: We have known enough of you. Now you are to know us!

HITLER WILL WIN, BECAUSE
THE PEOPLE WANT HIS VICTORY!

Munich, March 1, 1932
The National Leadership of the National Socialist German Workers' Party.'

SA and SS banned

Meanwhile the vicious street battles continued. The situation became so dangerous that it seemed that the army might have to be used to help the police keep order. Brüning persuaded Hindenburg to ban the SA and the SS from marching in public in uniform. Hitler, but not the

SA, accepted this without a protest. Hitler had no wish to be involved in another uprising like 1923. Since that date he had been determined he would become ruler of Germany legally and correctly.

Schleicher

After the 1930 election result, Brüning's position was weak. In particular the Minister of Defence, General Kurt von Schleicher, was determined that Brüning should go. Von Schleicher believed he could win over and 'tame' Hitler while Brüning saw the Nazi leader as a threat. In May 1932 von Schleicher succeeded in turning Hindenburg against Brüning, who was forced to resign.

Von Papen

The new Chancellor was Franz von Papen. He had little support in the Reichstag. He also had some strange ideas; he hoped to bring back the Kaiser to rule one day. In an effort to win over Hitler, von Papen agreed to lift the ban on the SA and the SS. During the month following, more than 100 people died in street fighting. Then at Hitler's insistence von Papen ordered new elections for 31 July 1932. During the campaign Communists opened fire on a Nazi march through Hamburg. Seventeen men died and 300 were wounded. Von Papen declared that the Socialist-ruled State of Prussia, in which Hamburg was situated, was out of control. He declared a state of emergency in Prussia and sacked its government. The Socialists left office quietly, fearing a Nazi uprising if they didn't go.

Nazis and the ballot box, 1932–33

July 1932 election

In preparation for the election of 31 July 1932, Hitler and his men organised a massive campaign of rallies and speeches. Piloted by the skilful Hans Baur, Hitler flew around Germany. Wherever he landed, he would be met by one of his two chauffeur-driven Mercedes cars, which covered 50,000 kilometres during the election. During the last two weeks Hitler spoke in fifty towns and cities. At Stralsund the crowd waited for him in the rain until 2.30 a.m. Baur had been unable to find a suitable landing place near the rally. At the Grünwald Stadium in Berlin, more than 100,000 people attended. Even more stood outside listening to the speeches through loudspeakers.

All the efforts paid off. When the results were announced the NSDAP had become the largest party in the Reichstag. 230 Nazi deputies were elected. Their 13.74 million votes was more than 37 per cent of the total cast. The Social Democrats got almost 8 million votes with 133 seats. The Communists came third with 5.3 million votes.

SA violence

Following the election a number of SA believed the time had come to seize power. They attacked and burnt out Social Democrat and Centre Party offices. Hitler realised that the army could probably crush any uprising but he had great difficulty in persuading the SA to be patient. Meanwhile, Hitler met General von Schleicher who supported his bid to become Chancellor. President Hindenburg however regarded 'corporal' Hitler and the SA with contempt. Only if Hitler would agree to co-operate with von Papen would Hindenburg appoint him as Chancellor. This Hitler refused to do.

November 1932 election

The election results meant that von Papen had no hope of finding enough support in the Reichstag to stay as Chancellor. He persuaded Hindenburg to dissolve the Reichstag and, at the same time the Communist deputies proposed a vote of 'no confidence' in him. It was carried by 512 to 42. This meant that by law yet another election had to be held. The latest possible legal date for an election was 6 November 1932. Von Papen chose it.

There was little enthusiasm for another election among the voters or the politicians. The Nazis were desperately short of money. Only five days before voting Hitler was upset to learn that his girlfriend Eva Braun had tried to commit suicide. This was the second woman who had shot herself because of Hitler; Geli Raubal, Hitler's niece, had killed herself in September 1931. More embarrassing politically for Hitler was the news that Nazis and Communists had joined forces in a transport strike in Berlin. They had formed joint picket lines.

The crucial weeks, November 1932-January 1933

Nazi slippage

The November 1932 election result was a disappointment for Hitler. Although remaining the largest party, the NSDAP lost 34 seats and 2 million votes. The new Reichstag had 196 Nazis, 121 Social Democrats, 100 Communists, 70 Centre Party and 51 Nationalists. Chancellor von Papen still had no hope of finding enough deputies to support his government and so offered to resign.

Chancellor von Schleicher

FEARED CIVIL WAR WHICH WOULD'VE RESULTED IN POLISH INVASION IF GERMANY WAS LED BY VON PAPEN.

Hindenburg had to offer the chance to Hitler, as leader of the largest party, to form a government. Hitler refused unless he was given very wide powers. Hindenburg said no and turned back to von Papen. Once more General von Schleicher became involved; he warned Hindenburg that a government under von Papen would lead to total chaos. He said there would be a general strike, an uprising by both Nazis and Communists and a Polish invasion. Hindenburg could see there was a danger of both the army and police being overwhelmed, so he then asked von Schleicher to form a government. Reluctantly von Schleicher accepted on the 3rd December 1932. His attempts to gain support were hopeless.

Conspiracy

CRUCIAL CHANCE MOMENT
POLICY OF KUHHANDEL

The path to the Chancellorship for Hitler was opened by von Papen. The two men met secretly in Cologne early in 1933. Von Papen hated von Schleicher and was determined to overthrow him. He suggested to Hitler that the Nazis and the Nationalists form a joint government. Hitler would be Chancellor but the Nationalists would have a majority in the government. Hitler agreed but on condition that the Social Democrats, the Communists and the Jews should be removed from important positions in Germany.

Von Schleicher resigns

Meanwhile Hindenburg and von Schleicher were hardly speaking to each other. They were arguing about the future of some large bankrupt estates in eastern Germany. Von Schleicher's position was becoming impossible; he had succeeded in upsetting everyone. Finally he decided he could rule only by setting up a military dictatorship. No-one would support this idea and on 28 January 1933, he was forced to resign. Now Hitler was the only possible choice for Chancellor.

Nazis in government

Talks were held amongst leading politicians. It was agreed that Hitler would be Chancellor, von Papen Vice-Chancellor, and Hugenburg, the National Party leader, would be minister of economic affairs. Only two other Nazis would be in the cabinet.

At 11.20 a.m. on 30 January 1933, Hitler and the new ministers entered Hindenburg's office. They were sworn into power. Thirteen years after he had set up the NSDAP in Munich, Adolf Hitler, forty-three years of age, took charge of the government of Germany.

Chancellor Adolf Hitler takes the salute of a guard of honour

PART TWO

GERMANY UNDER NAZI RULE

6

Gleischa' / Gleichschaltung
Authoritarianism
1932-33

From Chancellor to Führer

The Nazis in power *1st Revolution*

Not yet a dictator   Hitler was Chancellor but his powers were very limited. The Nazi politicians were only a minority in the cabinet and in the Reichstag. The civil service and the law courts operated independently. The separate German states *Länder*, especially Bavaria, had independent powers. Most importantly, the army had no loyalty to him. The generals were suspicious of the SA and believed it had plans to become a separate army. The other big powers, especially France, were watching him keenly. The source of Hitler's power was still the presidential decree.

For the first few weeks, Hitler treated everyone with care. He flattered Hindenburg. He tried to convince him that the Nazis were 'new Germans', young, strong and patriotic. Hitler held talks with the Nationalists and the Centre Party. He had dinner with the leading generals and admirals. He promised them he would keep the SA under control, crush the Communists and spend more on armaments.

In a speech to leading army generals on 3 February, 1933, Hitler listed some of his most important policies:

'1   Domestic policy: Complete reversal of the present domestic political situation in Germany. Refusal to tolerate any attitude contrary to this aim (pacifism!). Those who will not be converted must be broken. Extermination of Marxism root and branch. Death penalty for high treason. Tightest authoritarian state leadership. Removal of the cancer of democracy!

2   Foreign policy: Battle against Versailles. Equality of rights in Geneva [disarmament conference]; but useless if people do not have the will to fight . . .

3   Economics: The farmer must be saved! Settlement policy! Further increase of exports useless. The capacity of the world is limited and production is forced up everywhere. The only possibility of re-employing part of the army of unemployed lies in settlement . . . living space too small for German people.

4 Building up of the armed forces: Most important prerequisite for achieving the goal of regaining political power. National Service must be re-introduced. But beforehand the state leadership must ensure that the men subject to military service are not, even before their entry, poisoned by pacifism, Marxism, Bolshevism . . .'

Hitler decided there must be one more election. He did not expect the Nazis alone to win and absolute majority but he believed this could be done with allies such as the Nationalist Party. This would allow him to pass laws which would give him the powers he wanted. Meanwhile Hitler persuaded Hindenburg to sign a decree which restricted political meetings and opposition newspapers. Then Göring took over as Minister of the Interior in Prussia. This was the largest state and covered two-thirds of Germany. Göring quickly replaced leading officials, especially in the police, with Nazis.

Reichstag fire

Strong resistance to the Nazis was coming from the Communists. Then a week before the election the Reichstag building was destroyed by a deliberate fire. A young Dutch Communist, Marinus van der Lubbe, was arrested. He confessed that he hoped his action would be the signal for a revolution, yet it is almost certain that he was suffering from a mental illness. Several months later he was beheaded by an axeman in evening dress. Nazi leaders used the fire as an excuse to arrest 3000 leading Communists and Social Democrats. During the last days before the elections the Nazis sent out a stream of warnings about the 'Communist revolution'. Meanwhile money from industrialists had been pouring into the Nazis' election fund.

Rudolf Diels, in charge of the police investigation into the Reichstag Fire, wrote in 1950:

'. . . When I pushed my way into the burning building with Schneider, we had to climb over the bulging hoses of the Berlin fire brigade, although, as yet, there were few onlookers. A few officers of my department were already engaged in interrogating Marinus van der Lubbe. Naked from the waist upwards, smeared with dirt and sweating, he sat in front of them, breathing heavily. He panted as if he had completed a tremendous task. There was a wild triumphant gleam in the burning eyes of his pale, haggard young face. I sat opposite him in the police headquarters several times that night and listened to his confused stories. I read the Communist pamphlets he carried in his trouser pockets. They were of the kind which in those days were publicly distributed everywhere.'

Nazi-Nationalist majority

Despite all their efforts banning their opponents' meetings, the Nazis failed to win a majority. Their 17.27 million votes gave them almost 44 per cent. This meant 288 seats out of 647. However, with the Nationalist vote of 3.13 million they had a slight majority with 340 seats. Since the 81 Communist deputies were either under arrest or in hiding, the Nazis had a clear majority, and power.

The Enabling Law

The new Reichstag met in the Berlin Opera House, draped with huge swastika flags. The corridors and assembly hall were patrolled by uniformed SA and SS men. Hitler, dressed in SA uniform, was greeted by wild shouts and salutes. In his speech he promised to revive the economic and moral life of Germany. He said he would work for international peace but he also said that to carry out his plans the Reichstag must pass a new Act called the 'Law for Alleviating the Distress of People and the Reich'. It became known more simply as the 'Enabling Law'. This law said that Hitler could make decisions which would have the same authority and power as laws passed by the Reichstag. Only the Social Democrats opposed it. It was passed by 441 votes to 94. The Reichstag had no further part to play except to applaud Hitler.

From this date (23 March 1933) Hitler had increasing power to order what he wished in Germany. However, there were other centres of power in Germany such as the army, the SA, the courts and trade unions. Each would have to be dealt with in turn.

Destroying the opposition / SECOND REVOLUTION

Trade unions

Germany's large and powerful trade union movement was the second victim of the Nazi revolution after the Communist Party. Hitler declared 1 May to be a Day of National Labour. He spoke to thousands of workers and union leaders at Templehof airfield in Berlin. He praised them and stressed the unity of government and workers. Next day the SA and SS raided the trade union offices. Officials were beaten up and arrested. All property and funds were seized. Union newspapers were shut down. A Nazi-led 'Labour Front' was set up. This ensured that workers obeyed the government and did not strike.

Socialists banned

The other political parties were also soon abolished. On 22 June the Social Democratic Party was outlawed as 'hostile to the nation and state'. The smaller parties were 'persuaded' to dissolve themselves. The last to disappear on 5 July was the Catholic Centre Party. Ten days later a law was passed making illegal any party other than the Nazis.

The individual German states also lost their independence. Nazi governors were put in charge to replace the elected state governments.

Nazis only

There was little resistance. Most of the leaders of the other parties and unions were amongst the 26,000 locked up or the 60,000 persons in exile abroad. A few had joined the Nazis. Nevertheless, Hitler decided it was time to clear out from the Reichstag all the non-Nazis. An election was ordered for 12 November 1933. Only Nazi candidates were permitted and electors were allowed to vote for or against a single list of candidates. Almost everyone who could went to the polls. Over 92 per cent voted for the Nazis: Germany was a one-party state.

This is how a Socialist Party member resigned from the Party on 17 February 1933:

'I hereby return my membership card and signify my·resignation from the Party. I am and remain a 'religious socialist'. Under the pressure of circumstances the SPD, even against its will, will be pushed aside and into the methods of left-wing radicalism. On the other hand, pressure from the opposite side will grow. The only thing left for me to do in all conscience as a teacher, a Christian, and a German is to try to evade the double pressure and, as ten years ago, try to live for my job, my family and my books, without being a member of a party.'

'The Night of the Long Knives' 2ND REVOLUTION

Army v. the SA

Hitler still had one major problem. This was what to do with the SA, 400,000 strong, under the command of Captain Röhm. Now that he was in power, Hitler no longer needed the SA. Röhm, however, wished to turn the SA into a 'people's army'. The regular army would have the job only of training the SA for war. Hitler had no such plans. He respected the knowledge and skills of the generals. He knew that Hindenburg would oppose Röhm's ideas. So also would the British and French. They had no wish to see the German army become five times larger. The SA also wanted Hitler to bring in socialist policies. In particular they wanted the state to take over factories and steel mills. Röhm had many rivals: Göring wanted to become commander-in-chief of the armed forces; Himmler, the SS leader, wanted to increase his power.

Reinhardt Heydrich

Another enemy of Röhm was Reinhardt Heydrich, a former naval officer. Heydrich had been dismissed from the navy and had joined the SS in 1931. He became head of the SD – the SS intelligence service. Heydrich began spreading forged papers which claimed that Röhm was planning a revolution. Heydrich hoped to persuade Hitler that the SA leadership was dangerous and should be wiped out.

SA on leave

By June 1934 Hindenburg was seriously ill. Hitler was worried that when he died the army might decide to physically crush the SA threat. Hitler might be crushed with it. He was also coming to believe that an SA uprising was possible. Hitler met the Defence Minister and told him he would deal with the SA threat. The SA was ordered to take a month's leave from 1 July. On 28 June, whilst attending a wedding at Essen, Hitler received a telephone call from Himmler who claimed that an SA uprising would take place the next day. This was a lie – many of the SA leaders were on holiday at Bad Wiessel near Munich.

Murder of Röhm

Hitler made up his mind. He flew to Munich at once, collected an SS unit and drove to Röhm's hotel. At 6.30 a.m. on 30 June 1934, they burst into Röhm's bedroom and arrested him. Throughout Germany the police and SS moved in, arresting SA leaders. Other leading opponents of the regime were also arrested. About eighty men including Röhm, General von Schleicher, and Gregor Strasser, one of Hitler's Nazi opponents, were executed by the SS.

The death of Röhm was witnessed by the Governor of Stadelheim Prison, Munich:

'. . . Next morning (Sunday 1 July 1934) two SS men asked at the reception desk to be taken to Röhm. Zink, who was at the entrance, in view of the strict instructions he had been given, refused. It was about 9.30 a.m. When the two tried to force their way in, Zink alerted the prison governor and the green police [state police], who at once occupied the corridors and prevented any intrusion. The governor ascertained that neither of the SS men had proper authorisation. It therefore took hours of telephoning to check their papers; even the Reich Chancellery was rung up. When at last it became clear that they had an order from Hitler, the two murderers had to be taken to Röhm in the new building.

There they handed over a Browning to Röhm, who once again asked to speak to Hitler. They ordered him to shoot himself. If he did not comply, they would come back in ten minutes and kill him . . . When the time was up, the two SS men re-entered the cell, and found Röhm standing with his chest bared. Immediately one of them from the door shot him in the throat, and Röhm collapsed on the floor. Since he was still alive, he was killed with a shot point-blank through the temple.'

After Hindenburg /SOCIAL REVOLUTION

Death of Hindenburg

The SA had been tamed and the SS had become the major Nazi force in Germany. The army generals were pleased; they even overlooked the fact that two generals had also been victims. Hindenburg blamed the killings on the SA themselves. However, Hindenburg's life was almost at an end; he died on 2 August 1934. As he was dying, the cabinet passed a decree making into one the offices of Chancellor and President. Hitler's actual title was 'Führer and Reich Chancellor'. He automatically became supreme commander of the armed forces.

Loyalty oath

The Minister of Defence and the three commanders of the armed forces were called to Hitler's office and asked to swear this oath of loyalty:

'I swear before God to give my unconditional obedience to Adolf Hitler, Führer of the Reich and its people, Supreme Commander of the Armed Forces and I pledge my word as a soldier to observe this oath always, even at the risk of my life.'

By the end of the day every member of the German armed forces had sworn this oath. This made his loyalty not to Germany but to one man – Adolf Hitler.

Hindenburg was buried at the scene of his greatest victory, Tannenburg, in 1914. Less than two weeks later, 90 per cent of the German people who voted approved of Hitler as Hindenburg's successor.

Hitler greets the crowd from the window of the Chancellery on the day he took over as President

Two leading Nazi officials described how Hitler's personal rule worked:

a ... A Gau leader who had access to Hitler was politically more important than a Reich Minister who did not see his Head of State for years ...

b The higher Hitler climbed, and with him everyone who had access to him and who was in personal contact with him, the lower the Reich ministers who did not belong to these privileged people (e.g. Reich Minister of the Interior Frick) sank to the level of mere civil servants. The Reich Cabinet did not meet after 1937.

In order to keep oneself informed of Hitler's opinion at any time, it was desirable to have one's own representative on his staff. The Army and Navy had their permanent adjutants there. Göring (Head of the Air Force) had a General Bodenschatz stationed there. Goebbels often visited Hitler's quarters personally. Ribbentrop (Foreign Minister 1938–1945) ... posted his own man in Hitler's innermost circle.

7

The Nazi Revolution, 1933–39

The economy

Back to work

The greatest economic problem facing Hitler was unemployment. In January 1933, the official total was 5.7 million yet the Nazis had no detailed plans for dealing with the economy. The party's economic policy was vague. It was both anti-communist and anti-capitalist to attract the support of as many people as possible. Hitler was personally hostile to communism. He was also eager to gain support from the great industrial leaders such as Alfred Krupp. If the Nazis had any policy, it was that the party should be in control of the economy; of trade, industry, agriculture, the banks and of the workers themselves.

Four-year plan

When Hitler came to power the worst of the depression was over. Production was rising, world trade was increasing. This meant un-

120,000 men worked on autobahnen *in the 1930. This road was in the Alps*

employment had already started to fall. Hitler planned to make it fall faster. He put Hjalmar Schacht, President of the Reichsbank and the man who had 'cured' the 1923 inflation, in charge of the economy. This was part of the first four-year plan. Schacht's first scheme was to employ thousands of unemployed men on public works. These works included building new houses, military barracks and particularly the new *autobahnen*. These were motorways hundreds of kilometres in length which swept across Germany. Other men were employed planting forests and building dams. The Nazi Party itself provided thousands of jobs. Extra civil servants, officials, policemen and guards were all needed.

Women excluded

Hitler believed strongly that married women should not work outside the home. As early as June 1933 he offered interest-free marriage loans of 1000 marks if the wife had no job. Hitler was also keen to increase Germany's population. So with the birth of each child part of the loan was turned into a gift which did not have to be repaid. This plan increased the number of households; in turn it increased the number of jobs in house-building and making household goods. The population of Germany rose from 65 million in 1930 to 68 million in 1939.

Labour service

All young men and women aged 17–25 had to do six months 'voluntary' labour services. Most of the work was on the big schemes described above. The young people lived in barracks which were covered with Nazi propaganda.

German lawyers had to spend time in a labour camp before they qualified

A Socialist Party Report described life in a Labour Service Camp:

'Saxony, April/May 1938: The daily programme of the Labour Service Camp at Beiersfeld/Erzgebirge 9/165 looks like this: 4.45 a.m. get up. 4.50 gymnastics. 5.15 wash, make beds. 5.30 coffee break. 5.50 parade. 6.00 march to building site. Work till 14.30 with 30 minutes break for breakfast. 15.00 lunch. 15.30–18.00 drill. 18.10–18.45 instruction. 18.45–19.15 cleaning and mending 19.15 parade. 19.30 announcements. 19.45 supper. 20.00–21.30 sing-song or other leisure activities. 22.00 lights out. The day is thus filled with duties. The young people, who have been deadened by excessive physical exertion, have neither the strength nor the time for the slightest flicker of independent intellectual life. The wage is 25 Pf. per day. For that the Labour Service man cannot even afford a beer which costs at least 30 Pf. . . . the students and intellectually superior people are grouped together in separate troops. They get easier work and are not bullied so much as the ordinary working class lads . . . .'
(25 Pf. = 25p in 1990 values)

Re-armament

The principal means of creating jobs was through conscription and re-armament. In March 1935 Hitler announced that all young men would have to do military service. In August 1936 conscription was increased to two years. Hitler never had any intention of keeping the German army limited to 100,000 as it had been since 1919. He planned to build up a powerful army, a modern air force and a larger navy. This meant that millions of Germans would be employed in the armed forces or the armaments industry.

Unemployment in Germany had fallen from the 6 million in 1932 to 4 million by early 1934. By 1936 it was down to 1 million. By 1939 Germany was short of 500,000 workers! Employers sometimes tried to poach workers by offering higher wages.

Paying the bills

Schemes to end unemployment and build Germany's military strength were costly. In the first two years the Nazis spent 4 billion marks to increase employment. Dr Schacht, the economics minister, could not borrow money from abroad. Nor, remembering 1923, could he print more banknotes. Increased taxes would have been very unpopular. Instead, Schacht introduced 'Mefo-bills'. ('Mefo' was taken from *Metallurgische Forschung* — Metals Research.) These were government-guaranteed bonds repayable in periods of up to five years. Everyone trusted them. So they helped to expand the economy by increasing employment and production. Up to 1939 12 billion marks worth of Mefo-bills and strict economic controls prevented inflation.

Bartering

One problem Schacht could not control was world prices. Between 1927–1933 prices of food and raw materials such as coal had fallen by up to 25 per cent. After 1933 they began to rise. 75 per cent of Germany's imports were food and raw materials. By 1935–36 Germany was unable to sell enough goods abroad to pay for these imports. Nor did the Nazis wish to introduce food rationing to reduce imports. Schacht had to think of new ideas to deal with this problem.

One of Schacht's ideas was bartering. This meant Germany made deals to exchange unwanted goods for food or raw materials. Most of the deals were made with the countries of eastern Europe whose people depended on being able to sell produce from their farms to earn even a small living. The Germans drove hard bargains. Countries such as Hungary and Yugoslavia had to accept manufactured goods, such as cameras and optical lenses which they had little or no use for and send the same value of food, timber and so on to Germany. No money changed hands but the Germans over-valued their goods which meant they were putting an unfairly low value on imports from eastern Europe.

Göring runs the economy

By 1936 Hitler wanted to spend much more on armaments. Spending had already risen from 2 billion marks in 1933 to 11 billion. Schacht thought this would ruin Germany's economy. Within a year Schacht had been dismissed. Hitler ordered Hermann Göring, already in charge of the second four-year plan, to run the economy.

Göring believed that Germany should greatly reduce its need to import certain 'military' raw materials and food. In particular he decided that steel, rubber and oil must be home-produced. Only then would Germany be able to fight another war successfully. This policy was called *autarky* – self-sufficiency.

Autarky

A new steel-works named after Göring was built. It was designed to use low-grade German iron ore. Most steel-works used high quality ores imported from Sweden. Synthetic rubber and oil was produced from German coal. All these plans had only limited success. By 1939 Germany was importing one-third of the raw materials it needed. Oil production reached 18 per cent of total needs which was only half the planned target. Rubber production was more successful but German-produced oil and rubber were both more expensive than the imported supplies. The Hermann Göring steel-works failed to produce steel suitable for armaments until it began to use Swedish ores. Nevertheless, by 1938 German steel production was 22.6 million tons, third largest in the world.

The expansion of the German economy after 1936:

Commodity	(in thousands of tons) 1936 output	1938 output	1942 output	Plan target
Mineral oil*	1,790	2,340	6,260	13,830
Aluminium	98	166	260	273
Syn. rubber	0.7	75	96	120
Nitrogen	770	914	930	1,040
Explosives	18	45	300	223
Powder	20	26	150	217
Steel	19,216	22,656	20,480	24,000
Iron ore	2,255	3,360	4,137	5,549
Brown coal	161,382	194,985	245,918	240,500
Hard coal	158,400	186,186	166,059	213,000

*Including synthetic petrol

Göring also tried to make Germany self-sufficient in foodstuffs. At the same time full employment meant people had more to spend on food. The population was also increasing so this policy failed also, except in bread, potatoes, sugar and meat. By 1939 Germany was still importing 17 per cent of her agricultural needs.

The Jews

Boycotts and exclusions

Hitler had an intense hatred of the Jews. He even claimed that he was an instrument of God, stating 'by fighting the Jews I do battle for the Lord'. He said this at the start of a one-day, largely unsuccessful, boycott of Jewish shops and businesses on 1 April 1933. The SA stood outside these buildings trying to persuade people not to enter. President Hindenburg protested about Hitler's anti-semitic plans. Nevertheless, a week later, Hitler used the 'Enabling Law' to remove all Jews from the civil service. The minimum requirement to be considered a Jew was to have at least one Jewish grandparent. Many Jewish judges and lawyers, already the target of SA attacks, were also dismissed. Jewish doctors and dentists were banned from some work. Some weeks later a 5 per cent quota on Jewish students entering any university or school was ordered. Jewish university teachers were sacked. Then the SA held bonfires of books written by Jewish authors.

Stormtroopers picket a Jewish shop with a placard 'Don't buy from Jews'

In October 1933 Jewish editors were dismissed from the publishing industry.

The result of these measures was that 38,000 of Germany's 550,000 Jews emigrated in 1933. In each of the next four years between 20–25,000 left, mostly to Palestine, the USA or Britain.

Nuremburg laws

Two years later, Hitler moved again against the Jews. In May 1935 boycotts and violent attacks by the SA on Jews began. Schacht, the Minister of Economics, complained that these were damaging the Germany economy. Hitler ordered them to stop but agreed that further laws against the Jews were needed. At the Party rally in Nuremburg on 13 September, 1935, he made a violently anti-semitic speech and ordered a law 'For the Protection of German Blood and Honour' to be drafted at once. The next night he ordered another law on Reich citizenship. Further decrees removing civil rights from Jews were passed in November 1935.

These are extracts from the law for the Protection of German Blood and German Honour, 15 September 1935:

I.   1 Marriages between Jews and citizens of German or kindred blood are forbidden. Marriages concluded in defiance of this law are void, even if, for the purpose of evading this law, they are concluded abroad.

II.   Sexual relations outside marriage between Jews and nationals of German or kindred blood are forbidden.

III. Jews will not be permitted to employ female citizens of German or kindred blood under 45 years of age as domestic servants.

IV.   1 Jews are forbidden to display the Reich and national flag or the national colours.
      2 On the other hand they are permitted to display the Jewish colours. The exercise of this right is protected by the State.

V.   1 A person who acts contrary to the prohibition of Section I will be punished with hard labour.
      2 A person who acts contrary to the prohibition of Section II will be punished with imprisonment or with hard labour.
      3 A person who acts contrary to the provisions of Sections III or IV will be punished with imprisonment up to a year and with a fine, or with one of these penalties.

And from the Reich Citizenship Law of 15 September 1935:

I.   1 A citizen of the Reich is that subject only who is of German or kindred blood and who, through his conduct, shows that he is both desirous and fit to serve the German people and Reich faithfully.
      2 The right to citizenship is acquired by the granting of Reich citizenship papers.
      3 Only the citizen of the Reich enjoys full political rights in accordance with the provision of the laws.

II.   The Reich Minister of the Interior in conjunction with the Deputy of the Fuhrer will issue the necessary legal and administrative decrees for carrying out and supplementing this law.

The Olympics

The 1936 Olympic Games had been awarded to Berlin. The Nazis feared a boycott of the Games, particularly by the USA. They also feared further damage to the economy by attacking Jewish-owned businesses. So, during 1936–37, compared with other periods of Hitler's rule, the Jews were less harshly treated. During the Olympic Games, Berlin was cleared of anti-semitic posters. A few Jewish competitors were actually selected for the German team. Overall, the Olympics were a great propaganda triumph for Germany; German athletes won the largest number of medals. However, Hitler was not pleased by Jesse Owen's four gold medals in athletics. He was a black American.

Confiscation

By the end of 1937, Hitler felt ready to revive his anti-semitic policies. As in 1935 he did this with a violent speech at the Nuremburg rally. Following this, pressure was put on Jewish businessmen to sell up and get out of Germany. By the spring of 1938, Göring was planning to confiscate all property belonging to Jews. Further bans were made on Jewish doctors, dentists, and veterinary surgeons and 30,000 travelling salesmen were sacked.

'Crystal Night'

On 7 November 1938 a young Jewish man, Herschel Grynszpan, entered the German embassy in Paris. He shot a minor official, Ernst von Rath. Grynszpan had planned to kill the ambassador in revenge for the deportation of his parents from Germany to Poland.

Von Rath died two days later. Hitler was in Munich with Goebbels at a Party meeting when he heard the news. The two discussed the murder. Then Goebbels told the Nazis that Hitler would not mind if 'spontaneous demonstrations' took place in Germany. There was some confusion as to what this meant – but not for long. Later that night the SA, soon to be joined by the SS, began attacking Jewish people and their property. At least 110 Jews were killed and many more severely injured. More than 30,000 were arrested eventually and imprisoned. At least 840 shops, 170 houses and 190 synagogues were burnt down. Many more properties were severely damaged. Because of the amount of glass broken, the 9th of November became known as 'Crystal Night'. Foreign reaction to this outburst of violence was totally hostile. Germans were seen as a barbaric nation. Many leading Nazis were also upset – not by pity for the Jews but by the 25 million marks damage to property and the cost to insurance companies. Hitler may have realised that 'Crystal Night' was an 'own goal'. Nevertheless, more laws were passed discriminating against the Jews.

This is an extract from the diary of 17-year-old Hermann Bremser:

'9/10.11.1938. Reply of the German 'people' to the murder of the Embassy Councillor von Rath by a Jew. Throughout Germany, synagogues, Jewish children's homes and Jewish houses as well as furniture and possessions are being destroyed. Culture in the Third Reich! Foreign opinion everywhere is disgusted. History will remember the day as one of barbaric behaviour by the German population.'

Emigration

Germany's Jews were now without jobs, education or transport. Almost 120,000 left Germany in 1938–39. But despite condemning the Nazis the other Western nations did not want Germany's Jews. The remaining 250,000 Jews, mostly poor, were left in Germany and had nowhere to go. On 29 January 1939, the sixth anniversary of the Nazi rise to power, Hitler gave a warning of worse things to come:

'If the international Jewish financiers in and outside Europe should succeed in plunging the nations once more into world war then the result will be . . . the annihilation of the Jewish race in Europe.'

The Christian churches

Nazism and Christianity

It was inevitable that the churches would clash with Hitler. At first some church leaders saw Hitler as their defender against godless communism. Some continued to praise him to the end. But it took about three years for most to realise that Hitler, while perhaps believing in God, was totally evil and anti-Christian. Neither could Hitler tolerate the churches since basically the Christian message was quite the opposite of Nazism. He was not strong enough to seek their immediate destruction. That, however, was his long-term aim.

Roman Catholics and the Nazis

Hitler had a respect and admiration for the organisation and power of the Roman Catholic Church. He therefore sought a concordat or treaty with the Pope. This was signed in July 1933. The Catholic Church was promised full religious freedom and church schools and religious orders were given similar promises. In return bishops had to swear loyalty to the state and clergy had to keep out of politics. The Catholic Centre Party was then abolished.

Soon Hitler was breaking the concordat. Many obstacles, such as the ending of religious teaching in schools, were put in the Church's path.

Archbishop von Galen

When the bishops protested, the Nazis began attacking the clergy. In 1935 some priests were arrested on currency smuggling charges. In 1936 Nazi papers and magazines began publishing stories accusing members of religious orders of sexually immoral behaviour. Relations between the Catholic Church and the state became so bad that Pope Pius XI wrote a letter to be read in all German Catholic churches on 3 March 1937. It fiercely attacked Nazi policies. Archbishop Clemens von Galen of Münster became a fearless German preacher against Nazi policies. By reason of his fame, von Galen avoided arrest. Many hundreds of clergy were not so lucky.

A Nazi bishop

The Protestant churches seemed a softer target for Hitler. There was no one united Protestant church in Germany. Each *land* (territory) had its own. Hitler planned to 'capture' these churches and unite them under a Nazi bishop. By late 1933 he seemed to have succeeded with Ludwig Müller elected as bishop of the 'German Christians'.

Confessional Church

A group of Protestant pastors led by Martin Niemöller, a First World War submarine commander, refused to accept the situation. By the end of 1933, 75 per cent of Germany's 8000 pastors supported Niemöller. They formed the Confessional Church which quickly established itself as a rival to the Nazis' 'German Christians'. Hitler made Hans Kerrl 'Minister of Church Affairs' with orders to end this division. Kerrl failed. The Confessional Church was then made illegal and Niemöller and several hundred pastors were arrested and imprisoned. By 1938 Kerrl had control of the buildings and the funds of Germany's Protestants. He could not get control of all their minds. The Confessional Church alone protested against the Nazi treatment of the Jews.

Smaller religious groups such as Jehovah's Witnesses were treated savagely if their teachings contradicted Nazi ideas.

Martin Bormann, Director of Hitler's Office, explained why he thought Nazism and Christianity were so opposed:

'The Christian churches build upon man's ignorance, and are endeavoring to keep the greatest possible number of people in a state of ignorance. For it is only in this fashion that the churches can maintain their power. National Socialism, on the other hand, rests on scientific foundations. Christianity has certain unalterable principles, established nearly two thousand years ago, which have become petrified into a system of dogma that is even further removed from reality. National Socialism, on the other hand, if it is to fulfil its functions, must forever be brought in harmony with the latest results of scientific inquiry . . .'

The army

Pleasing the generals

Only the German army had the power to overthrow Hitler. Therefore he took great care in the early years not to upset the generals. The murder of Ernst Röhm and other leading SA men was committed partly to show that they could not become rivals to the army. Hitler's promises to expand the army and provide modern weapons also pleased the generals. They were given the first three armoured divisions in October 1935. Hitler knew also that if the generals were busy with rearmament, they would have little time for politics or plots.

At the same time, Hitler was taking steps to make sure the army would never be able to overthrow him. The first step had been the oath of loyalty to him which every soldier had been ordered to swear on 2 August 1934. As the army was expanded Hitler made sure that officers who supported the NSDAP were promoted to important jobs.

Controlling the army

The two most important posts were those of Reich War Minister, held by General Werner von Blomberg, and Commander-in-Chief of the army, General Werner von Fritsch. Von Blomberg was a keen Nazi but neither he nor von Fritsch supported Hitler's foreign policy. In particular, they believed his plans for conquest in eastern Europe were foolhardy. Hitler decided to get rid of them both. In January 1938 von Blomberg, a widower, married his secretary; Göring discovered that the General's new wife had a police record as a prostitute. Hitler decided that unless von Blomberg divorced his new wife, he would be dismissed. Von Blomberg refused the divorce. General von Fritsch was the obvious man to succeed von Blomberg as Minister of Defence. This time Himmler, Commander of the SS, struck; he produced forged evidence that von Fritsch had been with a male prostitute. Von Fritsch denied the charge. Nevertheless he too was dismissed.

Hitler appointed General Walther von Brauchitsch as army Commander-in-Chief. Hitler also gave him 80,000 marks to pay off his wife whom he was divorcing. Von Brauchitsch, who then married a rabid Nazi, was heavily in Hitler's debt. Hitler himself took over as Reich Minister and Commander-in-Chief of all the armed forces. General von Keitel was made his Chief of Staff. Hitler then promoted Hermann Göring to be a Field-Marshal – he was already Commander-in-Chief of the *Luftwaffe* (Air Force).

Hitler in charge

In one day, 4 February 1938, Hitler had dismissed the two most powerful soldiers in Germany. They were replaced by himself and men who depended heavily upon him.

The following morning the Nazi paper *Völkischer Beobachter* carried the headline 'Strongest concentration of all powers in Führer's hands'.

Teenagers in Nazi Germany

Young workers

Before 1933 the Nazis had called themselves the 'Party of Youth'. The politicians of the Republic were the 'old men'. The Nazi plan for young Germans was that they should be aggressive but highly disciplined and obedient. Most importantly the young were expected to work. 85 per cent of school leavers went into jobs which did *not* need higher education. By 1934 sixteen-year-olds in heavy industry were working a 48-hour week. They could be employed until 10.00 p.m. Holidays were 10–15 days per year.

At the same time young workers had little freedom to choose their jobs. However, vocational training and apprenticeship were made more widely available. Young workers were then allowed time off to attend trade schools – they could also have time off for Nazi Party activities. So the future which faced young Germans was one of hard work, training for a trade and Nazi indoctrination.

Juvenile delinquents

Despite the Nazis' commitment to young people, there was a decline in child health. Many diseases, such as diphtheria and polio, doubled between 1932–35. Heavy work, military training and too much physical training led to other problems such as flat feet.

Juvenile delinquency, which had been falling in Germany in the 1920s, rose steadily in the first ten years of Nazi rule. Forging of official permits needed for travel and other purposes was particularly high. The Nazis also tried to reduce smoking and alcoholic drinking amongst the young. They were also concerned about sexual immorality. For example, during the 1936 Nuremberg rally attended by 100,000 boys and girls aged 15–18, 900 girls became pregnant!

One policy used widely by the Nazis was to take children into care. The number in care doubled by 1935. Many of the youngsters were sent because of criminal or drunken parents. Others were sent because they were handicapped in some way.

The Hitler Youth

Another policy was to use teenagers to fight crime. This was the Hitler Youth Patrol Service. The Hitler Youth Organisation (*Hitler-Jugend* or HJ) had been set up in 1925. The idea was to develop Nazi ideas amongst the young. By 1932, when the population of Germany was well over 60 million, there were only about 107,000 HJ members. By 1939 it had reached almost 7.3 million.

The Hitler Youth had two organisations for boys and two for girls. Seven out of eight young Germans were in one or another.

MEMBERSHIP FIGURES OF THE HITLER YOUTH

	HJ (boys aged 14–18)	DJ (boys aged 10–14)	BDM (girls aged 14–18)	JM (girls aged 10–14)	Total	Total population of 10–18 year olds
End 1932	55,365	28,691	19,244	4,656	107,956	
End 1933	568,288	1,130,521	243,750	349,482	2,292,041	7,529,000
End 1934	786,000	1,457,304	471,944	862,317	3,577,565	7,682,000
End 1935	829,361	1,498,209	569,599	1,046,134	3,943,303	8,172,000
End 1936	1,168,734	1,785,424	873,127	1,610,316	5,437,601	8,656,000
End 1937	1,237,078	1,884,883	1,035,804	1,722,190	5,879,955	9,060,000
End 1938	1,663,305	2,064,538	1,448,264	1,855,119	7,031,226	9,109,000
Beg. 1939	1,723,886	2,137,594	1,502,571	1,923,419	7,287,470	8,870,000

and the BDM Werk (girls aged 18–21): 440,189

Abbreviations. HJ, Hitler-Jugend (Hitler Youth); DJ, Deutsches Jungvolk (German Young People); BDM, Bund Deutscher Mädel (League of German Girls); JM, Jungmädelbund (League of Young Girls).

Scouts banned

In 1936 membership of the Hitler Youth was made compulsory. This explains the largest increase that year. All other German youth groups such as the boy scouts, except one, were banned within eighteen months of Hitler's becoming Chancellor. The one exception was the Catholic Youth Organisation which lasted until 1939.

The Hitler Youth emphasised the group rather than the individual. The young people were told constantly to think of the team, the group, the organisation or of Germany – not of themselves. It was also hoped that HJ youngsters from rich and poor homes would mix together. It didn't work out that way.

**Training
programmes**

A ten-year-old had to pass several tests before being fully accepted into the DJ (*Deutsches Jungvolk* – German Young People). These included remembering Nazi ideas and songs, map reading, war games and collecting waste paper. During four years in the DJ, German children learnt other skills such as arms drill and bike repairs. At fourteen, boys joined the HJ and girls the BDM (League of German Girls) for four years. Both boys and girls learnt Nazi ideas and practised athletic skills. HJ members also had to pass athletic tests: running 60 metres in 12 seconds, long-jumping 2.75 metres (9 feet) and a 36-hour cross-country march. Boys also did more military-type activities. Girls practised more domestic skills. After seventeen the emphasis for girls was on health, grace and beauty to equip them to be future mothers. For boys military training and discipline were most important. This training included firing machine guns with live ammunition.

The League of German Girls parades through the Brandenburg Gate, Berlin, in 1933

School life

Boys first

The German education system had had a very high reputation for over 100 years. As in most countries, boys were more favoured than girls. Only about 10 per cent of university students were girls in 1934. The number of girls at grammar schools fell from 255,000 in 1931 to 188,000 by 1940. Hitler's educational policies cut even further their chances of a good career outside the home.

Nazi teachers

Teachers were very prominent in Nazi organizations. 97 per cent belonged to the Nazi Teachers Association. 14 per cent of teachers held Party positions such as HJ officials. To encourage teachers to think 'correctly', the majority were sent to one-month camps. All below the age of fifty also had to do compulsory PE.

Important subjects

PE became a very important subject in schools – to produce fit young soldiers. Other important subjects were History, with great emphasis on post-1918 Germany, Biology, which was racist, and German language and literature. Even Maths was 'Nazified'.

These two questions are from Maths text books of the period:

'Question 95: The construction of a lunatic asylum costs 6 million RM. How many houses at 15,000 RM each could have been built for that amount?

Question 97: To keep a mentally ill person costs approx. 4 RM per day, a cripple 5.50 RM, a criminal 3.50 RM. Many civil servants receive only 4 RM per day, white collar employees barely 3.50 RM, unskilled workers not even 2 RM per head for their families. (a) Illustrate these figures with a diagram – According to conservative estimates, there are 300,000 mentally ill, epileptics etc. in care. (b) How much do these people cost to keep in total, at a cost of 4 RM per head? (c) How many marriage loans at 1000 RM each . . . could be granted from this money? (d) A modern night bomber can carry 1,800 incendiaries. How long (in kilometres) is the path along which it can distribute these bombs if it drops a bomb every second at a speed of 250 km per hour? How far apart are the craters from one another . . .? How many kilometres can 10 such planes set alight if they fly 50 metres apart from one another? How many fires are caused if $\frac{1}{3}$ of the bombs hit their targets and of these $\frac{1}{3}$ ignite?'

By contrast Religious Instruction was reduced. By 1935 it was no longer examined; attendance at prayers was optional. In 1937 priests were banned from taking classes. The HJ and Nazi Teachers' Association both tried to get religious education lessons stopped.

Studying in school and membership of the Hitler Youth worked against each other. German children, at least boys, were encouraged to be aggressive, to exhaust themselves in training and to be generally bossy. In school they didn't have the wish or the energy to study hard, so HJ members often got poor school reports. Various methods were used to hide this such as special exemptions for HJ members.

The situation was made worse especially by 1939 as the 1933–35 'baby boom' began entering school. At the same time a serious shortage of teachers grew worse; many teachers had been moving into better paid jobs since 1933. Overall therefore educational standards dropped steadily during Hitler's rule.

8
Nazi Power, 1933–1939

The SS and police

Himmler's ambitions

When Hitler became Chancellor, he began crushing any possible opposition. All his supporters were very pleased; each group and each important individual in the Party expected to be rewarded. Heinrich Himmler and his SS, by then over 52,000 strong, wished to take over all Germany's police forces. In Bavaria, where the SS had its headquarters, this proved fairly easy. On 1 April 1933 Himmler took command of all Bavaria's police. He also set up a concentration camp at Dachau, to imprison anyone he thought was an enemy of Hitler.

The Gestapo

Prussia was much more difficult to take over. Hermann Göring was in charge of the government there and he had no intention of handing over his police forces to Himmler. Göring had realised that one way to become powerful in Hitler's Germany was to have a private army or at least a police force. He formed his private police force from Unit 1A of the Berlin Police Headquarters. Unit 1A was an intelligence unit which collected information about political parties and individuals. Göring increased it from 60 to 250 men and put Dr Rudolf Diels in charge. In April 1933 Göring had a law passed to separate it from the Prussian State Government. He named his force *Geheime Staats Polizei* (Secret State Police). A post office official abbreviated its name to *Gestapo*; one of the most hated and feared words of the twentieth century. Göring made one serious mistake in the first months. He also enrolled the SA as auxiliary police in March 1933. The SA went berserk, attacking Socialists, Communists, Jews and anyone they disliked. They set up prison camps and torture chambers in and around Berlin. Diels finally used police armed with machine guns to break the SA's power.

Himmler and Heydrich triumph

Meanwhile, Himmler, with the support of the Minister of the Interior, Wilhelm Frick, had taken over the police everywhere except Prussia. Göring believed that a revolution led by the SA was likely and allowed Himmler into Prussia. Himmler took over as Commander of all Germany's police forces. Heydrich took over as head of the Gestapo.

The two most feared men in Nazi Germany: Himmler (left) and Heydrich

Within a year it was over 600 strong. Heydrich then began to re-organise all Germany's policemen as part of the SS. He also tried to unite the criminal police with the Gestapo but with less success. In 1936 Himmler was given the title Reichsführer-SS and Chief of the German Police. The same year a law was passed to prevent the Law Courts investigating Gestapo activities.

The Organisation of the SS

Sicherheitsdienst (SD)

Heydrich's first job in the SS in 1931 had been to set up a security or intelligence service – the SD. He did this with great skill and efficiency. He built up secret files of information on leading Germans, including Nazi bosses. When Himmler took over the Gestapo in 1934 he decided not to unite it with the SD. The Gestapo were mostly professional policemen and many were *not* SS or even Nazi Party members. The SD were mostly university graduates in law and keen Nazis. Nevertheless, the two forces were soon chasing the same enemies; they were rivals. In June 1937 Heydrich told the Gestapo to hunt for communists and traitors. They were in charge of frontier posts also, dealing with people wishing to enter or leave Germany. The SD was given a wider field to cover. This included education, science and art, party and state administration and freemasons and other societies. Finally, however, in September 1939 the SD and Gestapo were merged.

Abwehr

Foreign intelligence was the responsibility of Germany's military intelligence service, the *Abwehr*, whose head was Admiral Wilhelm Canaris. He and Heydrich lived near each other in Berlin. They decided that the *Abwehr* should carry out spying abroad and counter-intelligence in Germany while the Gestapo should hunt traitors spying for foreign powers. The Gestapo became very skilled at hunting down opponents of Hitler. One method they used was informers.

> Every staircase now has an informer. This 'staircase ruler', as one might call him, collects the Winter-Aid contributions, runs around with all sorts of forms, inquires about family matters, and tries to find out about everything under the sun. He is supposed to talk to the housewives about prices and food shortages, he pushes into people's homes, he is supposed to find out what newspapers people read, what their lifestyle is like etc. Even old Party members have taken their protests about this snooping up to the Gau headquarters. Effectively, every tenant is visited at least once a week by one of these block wardens and is questioned by him. These block wardens then have to send in regular reports on their investigations to their Party office.'

Concentration camps

SS Totenkopf-verbande

The SD and the Gestapo were both ruthless hunters of Hitler's 'enemies' in Germany. It was the job of the 3500 men of the SS TV or *SS Totenkopfverbande* (Death's Head Units) to keep these 'enemies' locked up in concentration camps. A disused brick factory at Dachau near Munich became the first permanent camp, on 20 March 1933. The first commandant was sacked by Himmler and replaced by Theodor Eicke, an SS *Oberführer* (Colonel).

Theodor Eicke

Eicke was a brutal sadist who had failed in everything until he became a camp commandant. He set about organising the camp, drawing up harsh regulations and training the guards. He ordered savage beatings of prisoners, such as twenty-five lashes with a whip for stealing cigarettes. He could even execute prisoners for serious offences. Beatings were given not only to punish prisoners but to harden the guards and make them hate the prisoners. Any guard who showed pity or sympathy for a prisoner was, Eicke believed, a useless weakling. Although many prisoners suffered horribly and died in the camps, the purpose was not to kill them. They were there to work as slaves. At first they made SS uniforms and other articles but the labour soon became harsher.

Six camps

Himmler was pleased by Eicke's brutal success. He made him Inspector-General of camps so Eicke's organisation and regulations became the model for future camps. By 1939 there were six camp complexes including one at Mathausen in Austria, which fell under Hitler's rule in 1938. The other camps were at Flossenburg, Buchenwald, Sachsenhausen, Ravensbrück (for women) and the original Dachau.

The prisoners

There were about 25,000 prisoners in the camps by mid-1939. Few had been tried and sentenced by a court – the vast majority were simply arrested by the security police and delivered to the camps. 'Forget your wives, children and families', new arrivals were told at one camp, 'here you will die like dogs.' Apart from the Nazis' pet hates – Jews, communists and clergymen – there were three main groups of prisoners. Each wore a coloured triangle on their uniforms to identify them. The first were professional criminals who had served three previous sentences. The second were 'anti-socials'; these included beggars, tramps, gypsies, drunkards, prostitutes, homosexuals and the mentally ill. The third were 'work-shy' – people who had turned down two job offers.

Slaves

It was very difficult to be 'work-shy' in a concentration camp. As the camps grew in size so did the jobs done by prisoners. They broke stone in quarries and carried it on their backs to the top. Other prisoners used the stone to make roads and buildings. A lot of work was in forestry and agriculture. The hours were long, the work was hard and the ill-fed prisoners became exhausted. The guards allowed no rest – they used boots, truncheons, and whips without mercy. Many prisoners died of ill-treatment. Some committed suicide.

Power struggle

One man who kept a record of brutalities in the camps was the Gestapo chief Heydrich, who had men working in the camp offices. Not that he had any pity for the prisoners; in fact he wanted to take control of them himself. By publicising the 'law-breaking' in the camps, Heydrich hoped that Eicke and the SS-TV men would have to give up control. Himmler, however, believed Heydrich had too much power already. He also wanted to enlarge his own 'empire'. So he supported Eicke and the camps remained under SS control.

There are extracts from Eicke's Regulations for Discipline and Punishment applied to all concentration camps, 1 August, 1934:

'The following is punishable with three days solitary confinement:
– anyone who in serving his food takes a second helping without permission.
. . . with five days solitary confinement:
– anyone who sits or lies on his bed during the day without permission.
. . . with eight days solitary confinement, and twenty-five strokes to be administered before and after the serving of the sentence:
– anyone making derogatory or ironical remarks to a member of the SS, deliberately omitting the prescribed marks of respect.
. . . with two weeks' solitary confinement and twenty-five strokes
. . . before and after:
– anyone keeping forbidden articles, tools or weapons in his quarters or in his mattress . . .

Anyone who physically attacks a guard or SS man, refuses obedience or declines to work . . . leaves a marching column or his place of work . . . or holds a speech on the march or during work will be shot on the spot as a mutineer, or later hanged . . .

Confinement will be in a cell with a hard bed and with bread and water. The prisoner will receive warm food every four days . . .'

The armed SS (Waffen SS)

Leibstandarte

In 1932, SS units were set up to protect party leaders from the SA and to increase the power and terror of the SS itself. These units quickly began to see themselves as Hitler's 'Brigade of Guards'. One unit, set up in March 1933 on Hitler's orders, was the 'SS Headquarters Guard, Berlin'. Six months later it became known as *Leibstandarte Adolf Hitler*. It was a fanatical group sworn to defend Hitler with their lives. It was also the unit which murdered the SA leaders on 30 June 1934. Sepp Dietrich was its Commander. In December 1934 these units became the *SS Verfügungstruppe* (armed SS) or SS-VT.

General Hausser

The SS-VT became a heavily armed police force, very little different from an army. It was responsible for the *internal* security of Germany and the regular army for fighting *external* enemies. However to be as effective as an army, the SS-VT had to be organised and trained by regular soldiers. Himmler found a man to do this. He was a retired Lieutenant-General of the German army, Paul Hausser. Hausser was able to attract some high quality officers and NCOs into the growing SS army. By mid-1936 he had begun to organise the SS-VT into regular regiments. On 1 October 1936 Hausser was appointed Inspector of the SS-VT but he was not in absolute control. There was too much jealousy and struggling for power within the SS police systems for that. Even Himmler found Dietrich's *Leibstandarte Adolf Hitler* beyond his control. Nor was Himmler pleased to hear of frequent punch-ups in Berlin bars between men of the *Leibstandarte* and the regular army. This was probably because the *Leibstandarte* did only ceremonial duties. Soldiers mocked it as the 'Asphalt Army'. It had no battle training until 1938 when Hausser was allowed to begin work with it.

New tactics

Some SS-VT officers were opposed to being trained like the German army. They believed the old ways of fighting had brought defeat in 1918. They wanted their men to be trained in small groups as 'hunter-poacher-athletes'. This meant much less time on the parade-ground and much more time in the field developing skills and stamina. These included the ability to cover 3 kilometres cross-country in twenty minutes in full battle-dress and equipment. The SS-VT men had lower educational qualifications than the army and came from poorer families. What they lacked in experience and tradition they hoped to make up for in fanaticism – loyalty to Hitler.

Army–SS rivalry

The army watched the growth of the SS-VT anxiously. Having disposed of one rival, the SA, in June 1934, the generals now found a new one in its place. They told Hitler of their worries. Hitler responded by limiting the fire-power and independence of the SS-VT. Then in August 1939, Hitler placed all SS-VT units under the army's Commander-in-Chief. Once again it appeared the army had triumphed against a rival.

General von Fritsch, writing in 1938, days before his dismissal, anxiously noted the rise of the SS-VT:

'While during the subsequent phase, we managed to establish a good, in many cases, intimate, relationship with all Party agencies, this was not true of the SS. As far as our side was concerned, this may have derived from the fact that there was hardly a single senior officer who did not feel that the SS were spying on him. It is continually coming to light that, contrary to express instructions from the Führer's Deputy, SS people serving in the army have received orders to provide reports on their superiors. Unfortunately, these matters come to my attention in such a form that I cannot pursue them.

Finally, the SS Verfügungstruppe, which is continually being expanded, must create conflict with the Army through its very existence. It is the living proof of mistrust, towards the army and its leadership.'

The making of SS men

Allegemeine SS

The specialised units of the SS were only a small part of the organisation. By 1935 over 200,000 men were entitled to wear the SS uniform. It would have been many more if Himmler had not expelled some 60,000 'undesirables' during 1933–35. These 60,000 were driven out because of their criminal records, drunkenness, age, or unfitness. Many went because they were thought to be partly Jewish.

The vast majority of this 200,000 remaining were the *Allegemeine SS*, or general SS, which was named in 1934. It included many part-timers who could be called into uniform for special duties. They did crowd control at some big parades. By 1939 they numbered almost 240,000.

Himmler also tried to persuade rich, noble and important Germans to join the SS as 'honorary members'. Many did so, believing the SS to be the elite of the Nazis. Younger members of these important families joined for a career. By 1938 large numbers of the German nobility held high ranks in the SS.

Many rich Germans quickly realised that Himmler was becoming one of the most powerful and threatening men in Germany. So they formed the 'Friends of the Reichsfuhrer-SS' to pay protection money. Over 340,000 joined and paid large sums each year which Himmler used to pay for the increased costs of his SS units and other schemes.

Qualifying for the SS

Following the expulsion of the thousands of 'undesirables', Himmler made strict conditions before admitting new members. Educational qualifications were less important than in the army. Physical and racial qualifications were extremely important. Every SS man had to prove that he had no Jewish ancestors, at least since 1800. New recruits were ideally tall, slim, blond and blue-eyed. Not all recruits were, but could still be accepted if it was thought they would be good SS men. Once accepted, the new recruit faced two years of training and tests. If satisfactory he passed through each of the stages on a famous Nazi anniversary. The successful recruit passed out on 30 April, Hitler's birthday, and swore his oath of loyalty – 'obedience unto death'. He then had the summer to pass tests of sporting achievement and learn by heart a book of questions and answers about the SS and Nazism.

Service in the SS did not count as military service. The young recruit had to do his term in Labour Service and his military service in the army. If he did this satisfactorily he returned to the SS. Then he swore to obey the SS marriage law. This meant in effect promising to marry a 'good, healthy German girl'. Himmler hoped that they would all have large families. Few did. Finally he became an SS man.

SS courts

It was clear that the SS was seen as something very special. In 1934 Hitler declared that SS men accused of crimes could be judged only by SS judges and superior officers. Furthermore, late in 1935, Himmler decided that SS men could defend their honour by duelling. If found guilty of a serious crime, an SS man was allowed to commit suicide to avoid imprisonment or the firing squad. The most serious crimes, in Himmler's mind, apart from the obvious ones like treason or cowardice in battle, were homosexuality and financial corruption. These could lead to imprisonment in concentration camps, in which the disgraced SS man would probably be 'shot while trying to escape'.

Wewelsburg

Himmler's interest in spiritualism, reincarnation, astrology and mythology led him to follow the mythical example of King Arthur and his twelve knights of the Round Table at the castle of Camelot. He rented the ancient mountain castle of Wewelsburg in Westphalia from the local council for 1 mark a year. He then began spending large sums of money (13 million marks by 1945, equal to £13 million in 1990) restoring it. Each of the twelve knights was an SS *Obergruppenführer* (Lieutenant-General) and had his own coat of arms, private rooms and a reserved place at the table in the huge hall. They met regularly with Himmler to decide future policies and ideas for the SS.

In a speech to Hitler Youth in May 1936, Himmler explained how SS men were selected:

'The young SS candidate leaves the Hitler Youth at 18. That will mostly happen on 9 November. Up to 30 January he will do his probationary period with us and on 30 January, the anniversary of the take-over of power, will receive his provisional membership card. How then do we test him to see if we want him?

We require from him his personal medical certificate and his certificate of hereditary health, i.e. we investigate his whole family. If

Hitler's terror force, the SS

we discover any illness or defect in his family, he is regarded as unfit so that we do not notice only later, when he gets married, that some-one is mentally ill or has tuberculosis

In addition, there is the most important certificate – the family tree. It is compulsory for every SS man back to the year 1650.'

The law courts

New laws

'The law and the will of the Führer are one' Göring told a group of prosecution lawyers in July 1934. This might not have been totally true. However, Hitler had the power to make new laws without their being passed in the Reichstag. Many applied to single specific cases. For example, a new law was passed *after* the Reichstag Fire on 27 February 1933. This law was then used to prosecute van der Lubbe and the other defendants. Charging people in this way (retrospectively) is against natural justice.

Sentences

The purpose of Nazi justice was to punish severely anyone who seemed the slightest threat to Hitler's rule or to be harmful to Germany. It was an offence to criticise Hitler or his government. It was an offence to refuse work. There were so many new laws was that many people broke them without realising it. The Ministry of Justice had no room for them in prison. Five times between 1933 and 1939, it had to give amnesties to thousands of people who would otherwise have come to trial on charges carrying up to six months in prison. On the other hand, sentences lengthened for people convicted of serious crimes such as burglary and robbery. The number convicted of such crimes fell by 43 per cent between 1933 and 1939. Whether this was the result of longer sentences, the end of unemployment or the tight control of society in general, it is impossible to decide.

Hanged at 16

Another reason for this decline may have been 'protective arrest'. The security police could round up suspected criminals and put them in concentration camps without trial. Capital offences (incurring the death penalty) were increased by three to forty-three in the first ten years of Hitler's rule. The minimum age for the death penalty was reduced to sixteen.

The Nazi system of 'justice' did not rely simply on laws and punishments. It also began to take over the courts. This was done in two ways. First there was set up in 1934 the People's Court to try cases of treason; even earlier in March 1933 thirteen Special Courts were set up to deal with 'political crimes'. Eventually there were seventy such Special Courts. No one brought before them could hope for a fair trial.

Crushing the judges

The second way of taking over the courts was by persuading and bullying independent judges and lawyers. If this didn't work they might be sacked and replaced by Nazis. Jewish judges and lawyers were amongst the first to be sacked. Many judges and lawyers did co-operate with the Nazis, whether from fear or hope of promotion. However, many others were prepared to defend 'enemies of the state'. There were also prosecutors who attempted to bring charges against SS men for brutality in concentration camps or for corruption.

Propaganda

Parades

Violence and intimidation were the principal means by which the Nazis kept control in Germany. However, both Hitler and Goebbels realized that these alone might not be enough and they set out to convince the German people that Nazism promised them a wonderful future. This was Goebbels' task as Minister of Propaganda.

One way to do this was by public spectacles. The annual Nuremburg rallies were the most famous. The 1936 Olympic Games were another propaganda triumph. Huge parades were held to celebrate such things as the appointment of Hitler as Chancellor in 1933, and his 50th birthday in April 1939. People who watched these events could not fail to be impressed by the power and confidence of the new Germany.

Censorship

At the same time, Goebbels made certain that only one side of the story was told. He did this by censorship of press, radio and films. In 1932, Germany had 4700 daily (mostly local) newspapers. Total sales were about 20 million. The Nazis closed down or took over thousands of these different newspapers. Almost 1600 ceased publication by the end of 1934. Eventually less than 1000 were left.

A similar thing happened to Germany's 10,000 magazines and learned journals; half disappeared by 1938. Those that survived were required to print what Dr Goebbels told them. Naturally these papers became dull and boring. Sales fell steadily until 1939.

Radio

Radio broadcasting was expanding rapidly in most countries in the 1930s. In 1932 there were 4.5 million radio sets in Germany and ten years later over 16 million sets. Radio sets were becoming cheaper so by 1939 it was possible to buy one for about an average week's wages. The Nazis had total control of radio broadcasting and used it heavily for propaganda. Hitler made 50 broadcasts during his first year in office. To make certain everyone could and would listen, sets were installed in factories and cafés, and loudspeakers were placed in the streets. When not being subjected to speeches by Nazi leaders or to news broadcasts, listeners received mostly light music. There was no rock or pop music in the 1930s. The work of Jewish composers was banned and so was jazz because it was the music of American blacks. Viennese music by the Strauss family was played most frequently.

Films

Cinema attendances in Germany in 1933 totalled 250 million. This figure quadrupled in the next ten years. Most watched German films, of which an average of 100 a year were made during the Nazi period. Of these, half were comedies and love stories and a quarter were musicals or thrillers. The remaining quarter were historical, military, political or for the young. Goebbels had soon realized that people would never pay to watch *only* political films (such as 'Our Glorious SA March against the Communists'). However, even love stories could be politicised – the hero would be a Nazi, the villain a Jew. All film plots had to be submitted to Goebbels *before* production began. Foreign films could be shown but were often censored. This could be for a variety of reasons; one Tarzan film was banned in 1934 because of the scanty clothing worn by the hero and Jane!

Newspaper editors were warned in April 1935 by the Propaganda Ministry about certain photographs:

'Photos showing members of the Reich Government at dining tables in front of rows of bottles must not be published in future . . . Ministers take part in social events for reasons of international etiquette and for strictly official purposes, which they regard merely as a duty and not as a pleasure. Recently, because of a great number of photos, the utterly absurd impression has been created among the public that members of the government are living it up. News pictures must therefore change in this respect.'

9

Germany, Europe and the World, 1933–37

Hitler's view of the world before 1933

Revising Versailles

In the 1920s Hitler held to two main ideas about Germany's foreign policy. First, it should reverse the Treaty of Versailles by regaining all the lands Germany had been forced to give up, and by re-arming. Second, Germany should become the single united homeland for all Germans who had once lived in the old Austro-Hungarian and Russian empires. This meant the people of Austria itself as well as Germans living in Czechoslovakia, parts of Poland and the Baltic States of Estonia, Latvia and Lithuania.

Lebensraum

Such a new German state would have 85 million people and the lands they occupied would be insufficient to provide them with food and industrial raw materials. To satisfy these needs meant moving east into the homelands of Slav peoples such as Poland and the Ukraine in the USSR. Hitler called these desired lands Germany's *lebensraum* or 'living space'. His views about *lebensraum* connected with his hatred of communists. He hated them for their political ideas and because he believed that most of their leaders were Jewish. The Soviet Union was also the country which would most strongly oppose his plans to win living space in eastern Europe and the USSR itself.

Friends and enemies

Hitler therefore believed that he had two main enemies in Europe itself, the USSR and France, which would strongly resist any change to the Versailles Treaty. Outside the continent there were the USA and Britain to reckon with. The US Congress had refused to agree to their country joining the League of Nations or having any hand in backing Versailles. Britain, Hitler believed, was more concerned with her far-flung empire. He believed it would be possible to make some sort of treaty with the British to weaken any thoughts they might have of giving close support to France against Germany.

Hitler could see only two possibilities for friends and allies. One was Italy where the Fascists under Mussolini had seized power in 1922 after street fighting against socialists and communists. Hitler became very keen for Mussolini's friendship and was prepared to let Italy keep the South Tyrol, a German-speaking area which had been made Italian by the Treaty of Versailles. The other possible ally was Japan, whose naval power in the Far East troubled the USA and Britain. In 1931 the Japanese invaded Manchuria, the north-eastern part of China which ran up the Soviet border. This alarmed the Soviet leaders and gave Hitler one more reason for looking favourably towards Japan.

Hitler, Italy and Britain 1933–35

After he became Chancellor in 1933 Hitler began with a cautious foreign policy. His own position in Germany was still insecure and the country was still weak and without an army. The other world powers were very suspicious of the Nazis and in his speeches Hitler stressed that he wanted peace.

Withdrawals and approaches

However, by the end of 1933, he had taken the first steps towards a new foreign policy. He withdrew Germany from the conference discussing disarmament at Geneva because the other powers made it clear that they intended to keep Germany's forces very small. At the same time he withdrew Germany from the League of Nations whose members were opposed to boundary changes in Europe.

After these withdrawals Hitler needed to prevent the other powers combining against Germany. He did this by opening talks with them one at a time. To Britain, he suggested signing a non-aggression pact and a naval agreement to make sure that the two countries did not drift into war, particularly about overseas territories. Britain did not respond. Hitler then turned to Poland, which had been France's ally since 1921. In January 1934, Germany and Poland signed a ten-year non-aggression treaty. Each promised not to attack the other in the following ten years. Naturally the French were alarmed at the way Hitler had come to terms with their ally, but so were the Russians. They had been at war with Poland in 1920–1 and now feared that Poland might be allying with Germany against them.

Visit to Mussolini

Hitler's first attempt to win over Mussolini was a disaster. They met in Venice on 14 July 1934 only after much persuasion by the Germans. Mussolini wore a magnificent uniform and put on a colourful ceremony to welcome Hitler at the airport. Hitler wore a blue suit and a mac. He was uncomfortable and was thought by the Italians to be 'a strange freak'. Mussolini understood German, so had to listen for up to two hours at a time as Hitler talked non-stop. At the end of their meeting Hitler had promised Mussolini he would not invade Austria although he wanted it to be part of Germany. Mussolini promised nothing.

Murder in Vienna

Less than six weeks later, Hitler's promise became valueless. On 25 July, 150 Austrian Nazis, who had been receiving money and guns from the SS, rose in revolt. They broke into the Austrian Government headquarters and shot the Chancellor, Engelbert Dollfuss. Mussolini ordered troops up to the Austrian border.

Hitler didn't know what to do. Then Dollfuss died. Hitler was furious with the Austrian Nazis for striking so soon. He sacked the German ambassador for siding with the Nazi killers and sent von Papen, the former Chancellor, to take his place.

Mussolini meanwhile arrived in Vienna and offered his support to the Austrian Government. He accused Hitler of murdering Dollfuss and called Nazism 'a savage barbarism'. He called upon the other powers to unite to prevent Germany re-arming and starting a war. Hitler was upset and embarrassed. The murder of Dollfuss took place only three weeks after the killing of Röhm and eighty others. To the rest of the world, Hitler looked like a bloodthirsty savage.

An American reporter who was in Vienna in July 1934 described the murder of Chancellor Dollfuss:

'Officials at the chancellery told me the next day that they first thought a surprise military drill was in progress. The uniforms seemed genuine and the men were disciplined. Then along each tier of offices, rude voices shouted: 'Come out! Hands up!' Doors were battered down and the staff herded into the courtyard. The more prominent officials were imprisoned in a small room and told that they were the first batch of hostages who would be shot if the plot miscarried. A second batch was then chosen to be shot after the first batch. It became clear that the men were Nazis when the first thing they did was to open the telephone switchboard to get in touch with the German legation. And one rebel told a friend of mine: 'Curious, are you? In half an hour you'll hear all about it on the Munich radio'.

Immediately on disarming the guard one detachment of rebels went up the main staircase . . . to search the state departments, find Dollfuss, and murder him. There is little doubt but that this group was specifically charged with this duty . . . . Dollfuss was given no chance to escape. He might easily . . . have been captured alive. But the rebels had one aim, to kill him. They entered the building at twelve-fifty-five and two minutes past one at the latest he was shot.'

John Gunther, *Inside Europe*, 1938.

Saarland

In January 1935 Germany regained its first territory lost at Versailles. The Saarland was an industrialised region on the French border. Under the terms of the Treaty, its inhabitants were to vote on their future after 15 years. More than 90 per cent voted to re-join Germany.

German re-armament

Hitler's failure to move closer to either Britain or Italy did not make him pause. German re-armament continued. The German air force (the *Luftwaffe*) was increasing steadily and the generals told Hitler they needed a peacetime army, not of twenty-one divisions (300,000 men) but thirty-six (550,000 men). At the same time both Britain and France were announcing increased spending on defence. So Hitler agreed with the generals. Between 11–16 March 1935, he announced that Germany now had an air force and there would be conscription to build up the army to thirty-six divisions. In short, Germany was scrapping the limits on its forces placed by the Treaty of Versailles.

The Stresa Front

Hitler's announcement upset the other powers. On 11 April, the British, French and Italian prime ministers met at Stresa in Italy. They condemned German re-armament and promised to be loyal to the Locarno Pact of 1925. This had stated that the frontiers of western Europe would never be changed by war. The League of Nations also condemned Germany. Within a month, France and the USSR signed a pact promising to help each other if either was attacked without giving provocation. The USSR and Czechoslovakia signed a similar pact.

Anglo-German naval treaty

Germany, it appeared, was isolated. Within a month the situation began to change dramatically. In a broadcast on 21 May 1935 Hitler once more spoke of his desire for peace. He offered to sign non-aggression treaties with all his neighbours and said he wanted a fleet that would be only 35 per cent the size of Britain's. In London two weeks later a German delegation, led by Ambassador von Ribbentrop, met the British to discuss naval matters. The Germans stuck to the 35 per cent demand. Without consulting France or Italy, Britain agreed. The Stresa Front collapsed.

Abyssinia

Nevertheless, Italy remained friendly with Britain and France. Unfortunately while Mussolini wanted peace in Europe, he also wanted a 'safe' war. For years he had been boasting about the military power of Fascist Italy. Since 1932 he had been determined to use it in Abyssinia (known today as Ethiopia). In 1896 the Italians had tried and failed to conquer this country in north-east Africa. Mussolini wanted revenge as well as military glory and a new colony.

Failure of the League

Mussolini believed that neither Britain nor France would object. The first fighting between Italian and Ethiopian troops had taken place back in December 1934. The League of Nations tried to bring about a peaceful settlement but Mussolini wanted war. The League condemned him as the aggressor and Mussolini ignored them. On 3 October 1935 he launched a full-scale invasion of Abyssinia. The League again condemned Mussolini but its members failed to take action against him. Britain and France's foreign ministers even made a plan to divide up Abyssinia. This caused outrage in the two countries when it became known but there was still no firm action against Italy's aggression. Using poison gas, bombers and tanks, Mussolini's forces conquered Abyssinia and on 9 May 1936 it became part of the Italian Empire.

The main reason Britain and France did not act against Italy was because they wanted to keep Mussolini as an ally. This tactic failed completely; Mussolini was angry with Britain and France for not supporting his little war. He began moving closer to Hitler.

Hitler strengthens his position, 1936–37

The Rhineland

Hitler was pleased by Mussolini's war on Abyssinia and its effects on his relations with Britain and France. In the spring of 1936 he decided to use this for his own benefit. On 4 March the French parliament agreed to support the pact with the USSR. Hitler said this meant the end of the Locarno Pact and on 7 March ordered his army to march into the Rhineland. This was German territory, but under the Treaty of Versailles no soldiers or fortifications were allowed there.

Almost every leading German believed that the re-occupation of the Rhineland would mean war. Hitler was certain that neither France nor especially Britain would fight over this matter. He was right. Britain told France it would not join in military action. Despite a massive superiority in numbers, France and its allies did nothing except protest. Hitler admitted that the 'forty-eight hours after the march into the Rhineland were the most nerve-racking of my life'.

Hitler had won a victory for himself and for Germany. He called a Reichstag election three weeks later. Only Nazis were allowed to stand. Only half-a-million votes out of 45 million were cast *against* them.

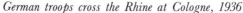

German troops cross the Rhine at Cologne, 1936

The Spanish Civil War

The event which finally drew Hitler and Mussolini together was the Spanish Civil war. It began on 17 July 1936 when a group of Spanish officers led by General Franco (the Nationalists) led a rebellion against the Socialist Government (the Republicans). Hitler and Mussolini supported Franco. The USSR supported the Republicans until late 1938. Britain and France declared neutrality.

There were several reasons why Hitler supported Franco. He needed raw materials produced in Spain. He believed a real war would be a testing ground for his armed forces, especially the *Luftwaffe*. He wanted to threaten France's southern frontiers by bringing an unfriendly government to power in Spain. Finally he hoped to drive a wedge between Italy and France and make Mussolini his firm ally. By late 1936 that seemed to be happening. Mussolini spoke of the Rome-Berlin Axis which suggested that the two leaders might sign a military alliance.

John Gunther described the changing European situation in 1938:

'Hitler's victory in the Rhineland, the victory of Mussolini in Abyssinia, the war in Spain, are branches of the same poisonous tree. Qualified as the victories may prove to be, they indubitably represent the temporary triumph of swift, hard-hitting Fascism against the slow motion and diffusion of power of the democracies. Mussolini's triumph was followed by Fascist forwardness everywhere in Europe, as those who had hoped to check him with sanctions had foreseen . . . Hitler and Mussolini may sometime come to conflict over Austria, but at present they represent almost identical dynamic forces. What is going on in Europe today is a struggle between law and right on the one hand, and the big fist and the machine-gun on the other. The struggle is between respect for international obligations and the most forthright kind of adventurers and predatory nationalism. The adventurers have won two important skirmishes. But democracy may have the final word.'

John Gunther, *Inside Europe*, 1938.

The Anti-Comintern Pact

In November 1936 Germany and Japan signed the Anti-Comintern Pact. The Comintern was the Soviet agency which tried to spread communism round the world and the Pact was clearly aimed against the USSR. It was one of Hitler's main enemies and had been hostile to the Japanese ever since they occupied Manchuria in 1931. Since then Japanese politics had followed a path close to that in Hitler's Germany. The power of the Japanese parliament had been weakened in favour of a group of right-wing politicians and army leaders. By 1936 Japan was in many ways a fascist state. Like Germany, it was also arming heavily and had become the world's third naval power after the USA and Britain. This gave the country's representatives the confidence to walk out of the 1936 London Naval Conference which was discussing ways of stopping a warship-building race. By doing this they roused the suspicion of Britain and the USA. The Anti-Comintern Pact was a way of breaking out of the isolation Japan had created for itself.

In 1937 Italy was also becoming isolated. The Italians walked out of the League of Nations which had tried, however feebly, to stop their country's conquest of Abyssinia. In September, Mussolini made a triumphal visit to Berlin and six weeks later Italy also signed the Anti-Comintern Pact.

Britain's concerns

The power most worried by the new friendship between the three aggressive states was Britain. Its government feared being dragged into European war by German schemes. Italy threatened British bases in the Mediterranean and the Suez Canal which was the sea-route to the empire in India and the Far East. The Japanese had become a major threat to British colonies and trading interests in the Far East, especially when they launched a second attack on China in 1937.

At the same time, Britain could expect little active support from the USA which clung firmly to neutrality. The USSR was not seen as a possible ally for Britain, whose leaders distrusted Stalin and were getting reports that his purges were weakening the Soviet army. This meant that Britain's only possible ally among the major powers was France, which was having serious political and economic problems. Neither the French government nor its armed forces believed it could keep Germany in check.

In 1933 Hitler had wanted a pact with Britain. By 1937 he had decided this was no longer necessary. Like France, Britain's economic and military power was declining. Neither country, thought, Hitler, showed any determination to stand up for itself. They were backing away from Germany's growing strength and confidence.

The Hossbach Memorandum, November 1937

Overheating economy

By 1937 Germany's re-armament programme was building up rapidly. It was having serious effects on the economy. Re-armament – building warships, tanks and guns – used vast quantities of steel and serious shortages were developing. There was a shortage of skilled workers and the cost of re-armament was growing rapidly. The building programme of *autobahnen*, stadiums and so on was also very expensive.

Hitler was faced with three alternatives. First he could reduce spending, especially on armaments. Second he could cut the living standards of the German people. Third he could take wealth and resources from other countries by invading them.

Conference in November

The economic situation was so serious that on 5 November 1937 Hitler called a top-level conference. The War Minister von Blomberg, the Commanders-in-Chief of the army (von Fritsch), navy (Raeder) and air force (Göring), and the Foreign Minister von Neurath, were all present. So was Colonel Friedrich Hossbach who wrote a report, which has survived and is usually called the 'Hossbach Memorandum'.

Hitler spoke at great length. Mostly he spoke of Germany's needs for more 'living space' and therefore resources. It was only by getting new lands that Germany could remain powerful and rich. Neither *autarky* (self-sufficiency) nor more trade could achieve that. To get more lands, said Hitler, could be done only by force. This involved risks, especially with Britain and France. However, Hitler believed they were weak and nervous about war; moreover, Germany had a considerable lead in re-armament. This lead would last until 1943–45. After that, the other powers would be equally well-armed. So, unless France had a civil war or a war with another power such as Italy, Germany must gain its new territories by 1943–45 at the latest.

First targets

The first of these new territories which Hitler wanted were Czechoslovakia and Austria. The map on p. 21 shows that Czechoslovakia was driven into the heart of Germany like a stake. Austria was the land of Hitler's birth. He had always believed it should be part of Germany. Once these two states were taken, the way would be clear to move further east in search of *lebensraum*.

This is an extract from the 'Hossbach Memorandum':

Case 1: Period 1943–1945

'After this date only a change for the worse, from our point of view, could be expected.

The equipment of the army, navy, and *Luftwaffe*, as well as the formation of the officer corps, was nearly completed. Equipment and armament were modern; in further delay there lay the danger of their obsolescence. In particular, the secrecy of 'special weapons' could not be preserved for ever. The recruiting of reserves was limited to current age groups; further drafts from older untrained age groups were no longer available.

Our relative strength would decrease in relation to the re-armament which would by then have been carried out by the rest of the world. If we did not act by 1943–45, any year could, in consequence of a lack of reserves, produce the food crisis, to cope with which the necessary foreign exchange was not available, and this must be regarded as a 'waning point of the regime'. Besides, the world was expecting our attack and was increasing its countermeasures from year to year. It was while the rest of the world was still preparing its defences that we were obliged to take the offensive.

Nobody knew today what the situation would be in the years 1943–45. One thing only was certain, that we could not wait longer.

On the one hand there was the great *Wehrmacht* (army), and the necessity of maintaining it at its present level, the ageing of the movement and of its leaders; and on the other, the prospect of a lowering of the standard of living and of a limitation of the birth rate, which left no choice but to act. If the Führer was still living, it was his unalterable resolve to solve Germany's problem of space at the latest by 1943–45.

10
Austria and Czechoslovakia, 1937–39

The Republic of Austria

The Rump of Empire

The defeat of Austria-Hungary in the First World War led to the break-up of the Empire. Austria became a small independent republic with a population of only 7 million of whom more than 2 million lived in Vienna, the capital city. The Treaty of Versailles forbade Germany and Austria to unite as one state. Many Austrians believed that union (*Anschluss*) with Germany was the only way they could survive and prosper.

Mussolini hostile

In 1933 the Austrians were more enthusiastic about an *Anschluss* than the Germans. Hitler in particular was more concerned about winning the support of Mussolini, who was hostile to a German takeover of Austria. In 1934 the murder of Austrian Chancellor Dollfuss by Austrian Nazis had embarrassed Hitler, not least because of its effects on his efforts to befriend Mussolini.

Schuschnigg

After Dollfuss, Kurt Schuschnigg became Chancellor. Hitler did not interfere with this choice and took steps to improve relations with Austria. In July 1936 the two governments signed an agreement. Germany recognised Austrian independence while Austria agreed to co-operate more closely with Germany. Austrian Nazis were released from prison. Two Nazis were given jobs in the Austrian government.

Mussolini's retreat

Italy supported Austrian independence up to 1937 when Hitler and Mussolini were drawing closer together because of the Spanish Civil War. Then Mussolini told Schuschnigg that the situation had changed since 1934 when he had backed Austria at the time of Dollfuss' murder. To add to Schuschnigg's problems, Austrian Nazis organised marches and violent demonstrations. On 25 January 1938, Austrian police raided the Nazi headquarters in Vienna. They uncovered a Nazi plot to take over the government.

Preparing for the *Anschluss*

Hitler had wanted an *Anschluss* since he was a boy. It was the first step in uniting all Germans in a 'Greater Germany'. There were other reasons. German re-armament was increasing rapidly. An *Anschluss* would mean that the Austrians would be absorbed into the German army. Austria had steelworks, lignite (brown coal) mines, iron ore and manganesite which would all help German industry.

Schuschnigg bullied

At his conference on 5 November 1937 Hitler had shown he was ready to move quickly against Austria. Early in February 1938 he re-organised the command of the army to give himself full control. Then he sacked von Papen, his ambassador to Austria. Von Papen visited Hitler and suggested that the latter invite Chancellor Schuschnigg to see him. Hitler agreed.

Schuschnigg travelled by train and car to Berchtesgaden, Hitler's home in the Alps. He took with him his Foreign Secretary, Guido Schmidt. Hitler greeted them in a friendly way. Then his manner changed; he grew angry. He accused Austria of treason and said he was going to 'make an end of it'. He shouted down all efforts by Schuschnigg to reply. Hitler then warned him not to try to defend his frontier with Germany. 'Perhaps you will wake up one morning in Vienna to find us there', he said, 'just like a spring storm', and 'nobody will lift a finger to save Austria.'

Seyss-Inquart

During lunch Hitler was a charming host. Later in the afternoon Schuschnigg was given a typed paper. It stated that Hitler would support Austrian independence but, in return, all imprisoned Austrian Nazis must be freed. All Austrian officials and officers who had been sacked for being Nazis must get their jobs back. A leading Nazi, Artur Seyss-Inquart must be made Minister of the Interior with total power over the police. Another Nazi was to be Minister of Defence.

Deadline

If he accepted these terms, Schuschnigg knew he would be signing away Austria's independence. Hitler gave him three days to make up his mind and also to get the consent of President Miklas and the Austrian cabinet. To help the Austrians make up their minds, Hitler ordered German army exercises along the border. Austria had no real choice but to accept Hitler's demands.

This was not the end of the matter. A few days later Hitler broadcast a speech hostile to Austria. In Graz, where they enjoyed the support of 80 per cent of the population, Austrian Nazis stormed the town hall. Schuschnigg sent troops there to restore order. To put pressure on Schuschnigg, Hitler then sent an envoy with demands which would increase Nazi control over Austria even more. Meanwhile fierce street battles between Austria's Nazis and patriots continued.

Der Anschluss

On 8 March, Schuschnigg decided to appeal directly to the Austrian people by holding a plebiscite in five days time. Every voter would be asked to choose whether or not Austria should remain free and independent of Germany. Hitler was furious when he heard the news. A victory for Schuschnigg in the plebiscite would make a Nazi takeover impossible to justify. After some hesitation, Hitler ordered the German army to be ready to invade Austria within 48 hours. The generals argued this was far too soon to be ready.

Schuschnigg's resignation

Hitler, encouraged by Göring, next demanded Schuschnigg's resignation. Schuschnigg agreed and broadcast it to the nation. He also announced that there would be no Austrian resistance to the German army. Thirty minutes later, at 2015 hours on 11 March 1938, Hitler ordered the German army to move into Austria.

Mussolini's support

After some resistance from President Miklas, the Nazi Seyss-Inquart was appointed Chancellor of Austria. To make the invasion of Austria look 'legal', Göring told Seyss-Inquart to send a telegram. This asked for German assistance to 'restore law and order' in Austria.

Hitler had not kept Mussolini informed about developments over Austria. Mussolini was very annoyed, but he needed German support in Spain. So two hours after giving the invasion order, Hitler was delighted to learn that Mussolini had sent a message of support. He was immensely grateful – 'I will never forget it' he told his special envoy in Rome.

German occupation

At 8 a.m. on 12 March, German forces crossed the frontier into Austria. Hitler followed a few hours later. First he visited Braunau, his birthplace, and then Linz. By midnight the first units had reached Vienna; thousands lined the streets to welcome them. Hitler was delayed by crowds and, much to his annoyance, by vehicles and tanks broken down along the roadside. He arrived in Vienna eighteen hours after the first troops. The following day he addressed a crowd of 200,000 and then, after a triumphal parade, he flew back to Munich.

An extract from Hitler's speech to the people of Linz, Austria, on the day of the German takeover, 12 March 1938:

'When years ago I went forth from this town I bore within me precisely the same profession of faith which today fills my heart. Judge of the depth of my emotion when, after so many years, I have been able to bring that profession of faith to its fulfilment. If Providence once called me forth from this town to be the leader of the Reich, it must, in so doing, have charged me with a mission,

German soldiers arriving to take over the Austrian army barracks in Vienna, 1938

and that mission could be only to restore my dear homeland to the German Reich. I have believed in this mission, I have lived and fought for it, and I believe I have now fulfilled it.'

Plebiscite

Hitler was determined to have the support of both the German and the Austrian peoples. He ordered a plebiscite to be held on 9 April in Germany and Austria. He then toured both countries making speeches and urging a 'yes' vote. Not surprisingly when the counting was finished more than 99 per cent in both countries said 'yes' to the *Anschluss*.

Nazi terror

One reason why so few voted against the *Anschluss* was the speed and efficiency of the SS and Gestapo. Himmler had reached Vienna even before Hitler. Eventually almost 80,000 'unreliable' Viennese were arrested. The vast majority were Jews; their treatment was particularly savage. Although many had already fled and others were released on payment of a ransom, most were trapped. A new concentration camp was opened at Mathausen near Linz. Prisoners were forced to do exceptionally hard labour in the stone quarries there.

Schuschnigg was also arrested. For seventeen months he was locked in a tiny room on the fifth floor of the Hotel Metropole. That was the Gestapo headquarters in Vienna. He was ill-treated and made to clean the guards' lavatories. Later he was moved to Dachau concentration camp but miraculously survived (dying in 1977).

The Republic of Czechoslovakia

Hitler's next target

Nobody in 1938 had any doubts about Hitler's next target. It was Czechoslovakia – another state created by the Treaty of Versailles in

1919. Hitler had hated Czechs since his early days in Vienna. He saw them as 'sub-humans' only slightly better than the Jews. Göring called the Czechs 'a vile race of dwarfs without any culture'. Moreover, Czechoslovakia was a parliamentary democracy, a form of government which Hitler hated.

Hitler saw the geographical shape and position of Czechoslovakia forming a corridor between Germany and the USSR. Through this invading armies might move and airbases could be built. From these, bombers could reach most major German cities within an hour or so.

Czechoslovakia possessed a strong army and had a powerful armaments industry. Along the frontier with Germany were strong fortifications. The Czechoslovak government supported the League of Nations and was also an ally of France and the USSR.

Clearly, in Hitler's mind, such a threatening abomination could not be allowed to exist for long.

The Sudetenland

Hitler's strategy for breaking up Czechoslovakia was to use the grievances of its ethnic minority groups. The total population of the country was 15 million. Of these only $7\frac{1}{2}$ million were Czechs. In addition there were $2\frac{1}{2}$ million Slovaks as well as 1 million Hungarians. More importantly, there lived $3\frac{1}{2}$ million Germans in the north-west part, known as the Sudetenland, which shared a border with Germany.

Konrad Henlein

Hitler decided to 'claim back' the Sudetenlanders even though they had never lived in Germany before. The Sudetenland German Party, led by ex-PE teacher Konrad Henlein, noisily supported Hitler's claim.

Since 1935 Henlein had been receiving money from the German Foreign Office. By early 1938 he was the undisputed leader of the Sudetenlanders. On 28 March he met Hitler and other leaders and it was agreed that Henlein would always demand more from the Czech government no matter what it agreed to. This would keep the country in a state of constant unrest.

The techniques were familiar. Henlein organised marches and rallies; there were fights with Czechs and with the police; swastika flags and posters appeared everywhere. In Germany the Nazi-controlled press and radio began a propaganda campaign accusing the Czech government of persecuting the Sudetenlanders.

Czechoslovakia isolated

Hitler gambled that, like Austria, Czechoslovakia could expect no outside help from its allies. France could only help Czechoslovakia physically by attacking Germany along the Rhine and Britain was discouraging such an action. The USSR was Czechoslovakia's other ally. Knowing that France was reluctant to fight for the Czechs, the USSR had no intention of helping alone. In any case Russian troops could move into Czechoslovakia only through Poland or Romania. Neither of the latter would agree to that.

Hitler in Rome

On 2 May 1938 Hitler, accompanied by five train loads of ministers, generals and officials, set off for Rome. He made several speeches praising Italy. He also let Mussolini know of his plan to destroy the Czechs. Mussolini seemed unworried about this and Hitler returned to Berlin very pleased.

Case Green

Czech resistance

The code-name for military action against Czechoslovakia was 'Green'. In preparation for this the German army began gathering its forces along the border. On 20 May the Czechs replied by mobilizing their army. Britain and France sent messages to Berlin warning of the dangers of war. The USSR and France both offered military help to the Czechs.

Westwall

Hitler had to back down; he was furious. Publicly he told the Czechs he had no hostile plans against them. Secretly, a few days later, he spoke to his generals and officials. He told them it was his firm decision to smash the Czechs and 'by no later than 1 October 1938'. He rejected the arguments by his generals against war and ordered a rapid completion of the 'Westwall', the fortifications opposite the French.

A troubled summer

During the summer of 1938, Hitler avoided direct involvement in the Sudetenland. He claimed it was a dispute between the Sudeten Germans and the Czech Government. Henlein was left to take the lead by organising strikes and demonstrations by the Sudeten Germans.

As the summer drew to an end, the Nazis let it be known that Hitler would speak about the Sudetenland at the Nuremburg rally in September. The British Prime Minister, Neville Chamberlain, feared this would lead to war. He decided that this could be avoided if the Czechs gave way. So, assisted by the French, Chamberlain began trying to persuade the Czechs to hand over the Sudetenland to Hitler.

Runciman mission

On 3 August, Chamberlain sent a special envoy, Lord Runciman, to Prague, the Czech capital. Runciman, who was sympathetic to the Sudeten Germans, achieved nothing. Hitler watched the increasing isolation of the Czechs with satisfaction. He encouraged the Poles to press their claim for the Teschen region of Czechoslovakia and made sure neither the Poles nor Romanians would allow Russian troops to pass through their countries to help Czechoslovakia. He encouraged Hungary to demand the return of its territory of Ruthenia in eastern Czechoslovakia. Hitler's main problem was his own generals; they told him that Germany was not strong enough to take on Britain, France and Czechoslovakia at once.

Sudeten uprising

Hitler refused to listen to the generals. He ordered them to be ready to invade Czechoslovakia by the end of September. Then he delivered a fierce attack on the Czechs in his closing speech at the Nuremburg rally on 12 September. However, he was careful only to demand 'justice' for the Sudetenlanders.

The effect of his speech was dramatic. At the border town of Eger (now Cheb) Henlein began an uprising. The Czech police opened fire and the government declared martial law. Henlein and his men fled into Germany.

A British reporter drove through the Sudetenland after the September uprising:

'We hired a car and left the next morning. A few miles outside Prague we passed three school-children cycling down a dusty road, their pigtails flying in the breeze, with long grey cylindrical gas-masks slung carelessly over their handle-bars. A little farther on the Czech lines of defence started – neat rows of pill-boxes, camouflaged to look like haystacks, that stretched for miles across the fields. They were guarded by Czech soldiers with fixed bayonets and steel helmets, who seemed oddly out of place in the peaceful countryside; peasants in nearby fields went on working as though their presence was a matter of course.

It wasn't difficult to tell when we had reached the Sudeten districts, for the white posts along the road suddenly bloomed with swastikas vividly painted with red chalk. The telephone posts blazed with "Heil Hitler" and most of the sign-boards bearing Czech names had been mutilated and torn down . . .

Ed and I drove for several hours; the outbreaks could scarcely be described (as the German press claimed) as "civil war". The quick action of the Czechs in declaring martial law had soon re-established order. Only a few districts still showed outward hostility. One of these was Eger, a town not far from the frontier. Here the Nazi machine was well organized and the community offered a grim picture of resistance.

We drove into the main square, which ordinarily hummed with life, to find it deserted. The Germans had pulled down their blinds, closed their shops, and now they refused to leave their houses. The streets were empty save for a few Czech gendarmes and stray groups of soldiers who stood forlornly at the corners. There was no traffic, only an occasional army lorry that came rattling through the square headed for some unknown destination. The Czechs had posted notices appealing to the people to resume their normal duties, but no one had responded. It was a weird experience to wander through the silent streets and to know the town was not deserted at all – that behind the drawn blinds the Germans sat waiting.'

Virginia Cowles, *Looking for Trouble*, 1941.

Chamberlain at Berchtesgaden

Despite the Czechs' victory, the French government was convinced Hitler would invade. France would then have to fight. Edouard Daladier, the French Prime Minister, suggested that Chamberlain should go to meet Hitler. Chamberlain agreed and so did a delighted Hitler. On 15 September Chamberlain made the four-and-a-half-hour flight from London to Munich, the first ever in his life. He then spent a further four hours on the road to Berchtesgaden.

Hitler and Chamberlain met for three hours. Hitler, as usual, did most of the talking. Eventually he said he was willing to risk a world war rather than leave the Sudetenland question unsettled. Chamberlain replied that if Hitler was determined to use force, his long journey had been a waste of time. Hitler changed course: he said if Chamberlain would agree to the Sudetenland being handed over to Germany, the only question was how. Chamberlain agreed to return to London for consultations about this transfer. Hitler promised not to attack Czechoslovakia, meanwhile, unless 'something atrocious' happened.

The British Ambassador to Berlin recalled the Hitler-Chamberlain meeting at Berchtesgaden in September 1938:

'The first item on the programme was tea, which was served in a semi-circle before the fireplace situated opposite the great window of the reception-room looking across the mountains to Salzburg. After twenty minutes of desultory conversation, the Chancellor suggested to the Prime Minister that they might begin their talk, and they disappeared together with the reliable interpreter, Dr Schmidt, into Hitler's study . . . .

In the course of this first conversation, which lasted for three hours, Hitler made it clear that the only terms on which he could agree to a peaceful solution by agreement were on the basis of the acceptance of the principle of self-determination. The Prime Minister finally accepted that principle for himself, and undertook to consult his cabinet and to endeavour to secure its consent to it, and likewise that of the French and Czech governments. Hitler, for his part, declared his readiness to discuss thereafter ways and means, and undertook to meet Mr Chamberlain again at a date to be agreed upon between them.

The Prime Minister accordingly left by air again for London on the following morning.'

Sir Nevile Henderson, *Failure of a Mission*, 1940.

Chamberlain at Bad Godesberg

Hitler's promise did not stop military preparations along the Czech border. Five armies totalling 500,000 men were assembled. The 'ethnic minority' problems continued. The Slovakian People's Party demanded home rule from Prague. The Poles and Hungarians demanded 'their' pieces of the country. On 22 September, Sudeten Nazis, armed by the Germans, seized control of the border towns of Eger and Asch.

On that same day Chamberlain flew back to Germany. This time he landed at Cologne where an SS band playing 'God Save the King' welcomed him. Then he was driven 40 kilometres south along the Rhine to Bad Godesberg. He was in a good mood. He had persuaded the British, French and Czech governments to agree to the handover of the Sudetenland. Nor would the people in this region be allowed to vote on it. All areas where 50 per cent or more of the population was German would be handed over to Hitler.

Hitler's change of mind

Chamberlain told Hitler of these agreements. Hitler then said that 'after the events of the last few days, this solution is no longer any use'.

Chamberlain sat angrily listening to Hitler's excuses. Then Hitler demanded the immediate withdrawal of the Czechs from areas which he indicated on a large map. These areas were to be occupied by German forces by 1 October if war was to be avoided.

Hitler wanted more than just the Sudetenland. He wanted to destroy the Czechoslovak state. He believed that all he had to do was hold out and keep threatening. Czechoslovakia would collapse as Slovaks, Hungarians, Poles and Germans each claimed their share.

Chamberlain and Hitler met again late next evening and once again they argued bitterly. Finally Hitler showed Chamberlain a map. He demanded complete Czech withdrawal from the areas shown by the 26th, two days later, and German occupation by the 28th. Chamberlain and his officials bitterly attacked this proposal.

Czech mobilisation

Whilst the arguments continued, news was brought that the Czech army was mobilising; Hitler said that this meant war. Chamberlain said he was returning to London. Hitler said he would allow the Czechs until 1 October to evacuate the territories he wanted. He then thanked Chamberlain, and earnestly assured him this was 'his last territorial demand in Europe'.

Threats of war

Letter to Hitler

Chamberlain had discussions in London with the cabinet, the French and the Czech ambassador. Finally he decided to write a personal letter to Hitler. He wrote that while the Czechs had rejected the Bad Godesberg proposals, war could still be avoided. He suggested a meeting between the German and Czech governments with British representatives present. Hitler listened to the contents of the letter and then left to give a major speech at the Berlin Sportspalast. It was a masterpiece of hatred and lies. When he finally got round to the Sudeten question he announced that 'My patience is at an end . . . Give the (Sudeten) Germans their freedom, or we will go and fetch this freedom for ourselves.'

Chamberlain's broadcast

The next day (27 September 1938) Chamberlain went to Broadcasting House. His attitude to Czechoslovakia was summed up in one memorable sentence. 'How horrible, how fantastic, how incredible it is that we should be trying on gas masks here because of a quarrel in a faraway country between people of whom we know nothing.' However, he did go on to say that if any nation was trying to dominate the world by force . . . 'it must be resisted.'

A letter from Hitler

Two hours after his broadcast, Chamberlain received a letter from Hitler. Possibly Hitler was worried by news that the French army and the British fleet were mobilising for war. Whatever the reason, Chamberlain decided on one last effort. He wrote to Mussolini and asked the Italian dictator to use his influence with Hitler.

Mussolini's armies were bogged down in Spain. He was very worried about a general war in Europe because Italy was in no condition to fight. So he sent a message to Hitler through the Italian ambassador in Berlin. He told Hitler that Chamberlain's idea of an international conference should be accepted. Hitler in turn was worried by the lack of enthusiasm in Germany for a war and so said yes to a conference if Mussolini would come. Mussolini agreed and suggested it should be in Munich.

The Munich Conference

The meeting

The conference was arranged for 29 September in the Führerbau in Munich's Königsplatz. Hitler sent invitations to Chamberlain, Daladier and Mussolini. No Czechs or Russians were invited. Chamberlain and Daladier flew in and Mussolini travelled from Rome in his private train which picked up Hitler and his party south of Munich.

The conference was ill-prepared. There was no chairman, no agenda and no organisation. Often it turned into a series of individual discussions. The official interpreter Paul Schmidt had an impossible task; often several people were speaking at once in different languages. Only Mussolini had a working knowledge of English, French and German. Therefore he dominated the proceedings.

Arriving at Munich: Göring, Ciano (Italian foreign minister), Hitler and Mussolini

Agreement

The conference lasted from 12.45 p.m. on 29 October until the early hours of the 30th. Neither Chamberlain nor Daladier were prepared to stand up for the Czechs. The final agreement called for the Czechs to begin withdrawing from the Sudetenland on the following day, 1 October.

'Peace in our time'

Chamberlain and Daladier had the unpleasant task of informing the Czech representatives at 2.15 a.m., of the break-up of their country. Later that morning Chamberlain drove to see Hitler bearing a document which he asked Hitler to sign. It was a promise by Britain and Germany never to go to war. Chamberlain then flew back to London. Throughout the world he was hailed as the saviour of the peace. In the House of Commons, Chamberlain's action was approved by 366 votes to 144. Winston Churchill, a backbench Conservative MP, said 'it is a great defeat without war . . . This is only the beginning of the reckoning'. Churchill and thirty-four other MPs abstained from the vote.

Munich – right or wrong?

Since 1938 the decision of Britain and France to force the surrender of the Sudetenland has been fiercely debated. The question centres on Hitler's intentions; whether he was determined to have the Sudetenland at any price. If he was, then Britain and France saved Europe, if only temporarily, from war. They saved the Czechs from much bloodshed and destruction. In the year after Munich, Britain and France were able to increase their own re-armaments programmes and so they were better prepared when war came.

However, the price of peace in 1938 was high. Hitler's popularity rose even higher in Germany. Since 1935 he had increased the Reich by 25 per cent in area and 16 per cent in population. His confidence and determination to get *lebensraum* also grew. The seizure of the Sudetenland removed Czechoslovakia as a potential threat to Germany. Hitler's contempt for Britain and France increased. If they had a year extra to re-arm so also did Germany.

Stalin's distrust of the western powers also increased. In surrendering the Sudetenland they were, he believed, pointing Germany towards the USSR. The French-USSR Pact had little meaning after Munich.

This is an extract from the Munich Agreement of 30 September 1938, destined to cause so much future debate:

'Germany, the United Kingdom, France and Italy, taking into consideration the agreement which has already been reached in principle for the cession to Germany of the Sudeten German territory, have agreed on the following terms and conditions governing the said cession and the measures consequent thereon, and by this agreement they each hold themselves responsible for the steps necessary to secure fulfilment:

1 The evacuation shall begin on 1 October.
2 The United Kingdom, France and Italy agree that the evacuation of the territory shall be completed by 10 October, without any

existing installations having been destroyed and that the Czechoslovak Government shall be held responsible for carrying out the evacuation without damage to the said installations.

3 The conditions governing the evacuation shall be laid down in detail by an international commission composed of representatives of Germany, the United Kingdom, France, Italy and Czechoslovakia.

4 The occupation by stages of the predominantly German territory by German troops shall begin on 1 October. The four territories marked on the attached map will be occupied by German troops in the following order: The territory marked No. I on 1 and 2 October, the territory marked No. II on 2 and 3 October, the territory marked No. III on 3, 4 and 5 October, the territory marked No. IV on 6 and 7 October. The remaining territory of preponderantly German character shall be ascertained by the aforesaid international commission forthwith and shall be occupied by German troops by 10 October.'

The final destruction of Czechoslovakia

Czech losses

Czechoslovakia lost not only its frontier fortifications and important industrial areas. Its rail system was disrupted now that it was crossed by a new frontier with Germany. Some 800,000 Czechs living in the Sudetenland were forced to become subjects of Hitler.

On 10 October, Poland took over the Teschen district of Czechoslovakia. At Hitler's insistence, the eastern regions of Slovakia and Ruthenia were given self-government. This left only Bohemia and Moravia, the two main Czech provinces, under the direct rule of the Prague Government.

Despite these drastic changes Hitler was determined to destroy what remained of Czechoslovakia. It was not simply a question of his racial hatred; he wanted the wealth of the country: its great Skoda armament works, the Czech army's equipment and the country's gold and foreign currency reserves. In addition, the agricultural output would help to reduce Germany's food imports. The only question which remained was when Germany would strike.

Slovakia, the key

Hitler issued orders to the army for the final destruction of Czechoslovakia less than a month after the Munich Conference. Further orders were issued on 17 December 1938.

A fierce propaganda campaign was launched against the Czechs in February 1939. They were accused of terrorising both their German and Slovak citizens. In Slovakia demands for total independence grew. President Hacha of Czechoslovakia replied by dismissing the regional government of Slovakia and sending in troops.

Hitler ordered the dismissed Slovak leader, Josef Tiso, to come to Berlin on 13 March 1939. He told Tiso that soon the German army would move into Bohemia and Moravia but that the Germans would not interfere with an independent Slovakia. Tiso returned home and declared independence. Neither Britain, France nor the USSR reacted.

President Hacha

In despair, President Hacha requested a meeting with Hitler. This was agreed and he boarded a train on 14 March for the 300-kilometres journey to Berlin. Hacha pleaded with Hitler to show mercy to Czechoslovakia but he was ignored. Hitler told Hacha that the invasion of his country would begin in six hours time. If there was any resistance, Prague – a beautiful, historic city – would be bombed. Hacha fainted. When he was revived he was advised to phone Prague and tell his colleagues not to fight. After some resistance, Hacha signed the document of surrender at 4 a.m. on 15 March 1939.

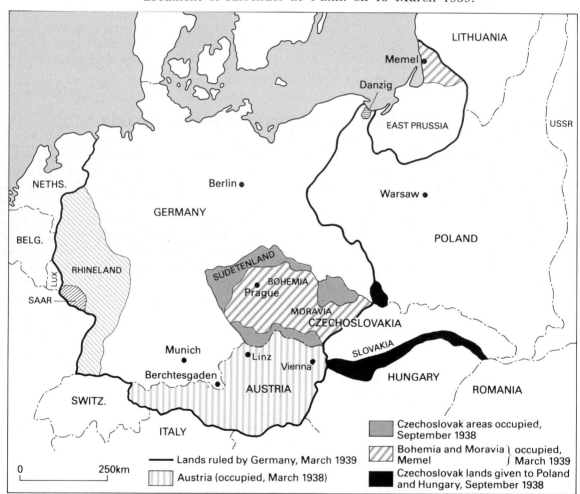

Germany's gains, 1933–March 1939

Occupation

The German army marched in a few hours later. Hitler travelled by train to the border. He then transferred to an open Mercedes and his convoy reached Prague the same evening. The occupation and final destruction of the Czech state was achieved peacefully. A 'Protectorate of Bohemia and Moravia' was set up. Konrad Henlein was rewarded by being made head of the civil administration.

The newly 'independent' Slovakia was taken under German protection. It became virtually a colony of Germany. Hungary was permitted to take over Ruthenia, the easternmost part of Czechoslovakia.

The result of Munich: Hitler's troops enter the Sudetenland greeted by some of its German people

11

Poland and the 'Phoney War', 1939–40

Britain and Poland

Chamberlain betrayed

The speed with which Hitler dismantled the remains of Czechoslovakia astonished the world. By the time the British and French ambassadors in Berlin had delivered their protests it was all over. Mussolini had learned of Hitler's plans only hours before they happened. There was nothing he could do to restrain Hitler. He was by then totally dependent on Germany unless he drastically changed Italian policies.

Chamberlain felt betrayed by Hitler. He had trusted him at Munich. Now Hitler had made him look foolish and inept. The British Foreign Secretary, Lord Halifax, told Chamberlain that the time had come for Britain to make a stand. Chamberlain agreed.

Guarantee to Poland

On 18 March 1939, speaking in his home town of Birmingham, Chamberlain changed the course of British foreign policy. He warned that Britain, despite its detestation of war, would use all its power to resist a challenge if it were made. Less than two weeks later, in the Commons, Chamberlain made a dramatic statement. Britain was offering an unconditional guarantee to Poland if its independence was threatened. Two weeks later the same offer was made to Romania and Greece.

The British ambassador to Berlin in 1939 explained why Britain 'guaranteed' Poland:

'. . . so long as German action had been confined to predominantly German areas, the British nation, in spite of its profound disgust at the methods employed by Hitlerism, had not been inclined actively to intervene. A preventive war for the sole object of hindering the unity of Greater Germany on a national basis would never have been tolerated either by the nation or by the Empire. No British statesman could ever have failed to take this consideration into account. But even the profound love of peace of the British nation would not permit it to tolerate the absorption by Germany of one independent country after another. The world has been taken by surprise on

March 15th, but there must be no more surprises. War would be the inevitable outcome of the next aggression by Germany. If Hitler wanted peace he knew how to ensure it; if he wanted war, he knew equally well what would bring it about. The choice lay with him and in the end the entire responsibility for war was his.'

Sir Nevile Henderson, *Failure of a Mission*, 1940.

The Polish question

The Polish Corridor

Poland was recreated at the Treaty of Versailles. During the previous 124 years its territories had been shared out between Russia, Austria, Hungary and Prussia. The new Poland recovered its old territories and some extra lands which had been settled by Germans. Poland was also given access to the Baltic Sea by a strip of land known as the 'Polish Corridor', which meant that the German province of East Prussia was separated from the rest of Germany. The main port in the corridor was Danzig, where most of the inhabitants were German but the Poles had special privileges.

Wooing the Poles

Hitler wanted Danzig returned to Germany. However, he had not pressed his claims at first. He had treated the Poles in a friendly way. If he had to have a war with France, he wanted to keep her ally, Poland, neutral. So in 1934 he had signed the ten-year non-aggression treaty with Poland. Nevertheless, Hitler's long term aim was to make Poland into a German colony. He wanted Polish soldiers to fight against the USSR and Polish farmers to help feed Germany's growing population.

Threatening the Poles

After the Munich agreement, the Poles were rewarded with the Teschen district of Czechoslovakia. Then Hitler asked the Poles to return Danzig to Germany and for a road and rail link between Germany and East Prussia. This link would be totally under German control. Colonel Jozef Beck, Poland's Foreign Minister, visited Hitler in January 1939 and refused even to discuss the return of Danzig.

The British guarantee to Poland on 31 March 1939 changed completely Hitler's attitude to the Poles. He knew that the Poles now felt no need to keep him friendly. Four days after the guarantee offer, Hitler ordered the army to prepare plans for 'Operation White' to invade Poland on 1 September 1939.

Colonel Beck arrived in London on 5 April to discuss the treaty with the British. During talks, Chamberlain made a suggestion that Poland and the two Western powers should join with the USSR against Germany. Colonel Beck refused absolutely to consider this.

Hitler was more angry with the British than the Poles. He resented bitterly Britain's 'interference' in east European affairs. He was, he said, quite prepared for war with Britain and warned the British that such a war would be 'unimaginably destructive'.

Roosevelt's letter   Whilst the world's attention was on Poland, Mussolini invaded Albania, a small, mountainous country between Greece and Yugoslavia, on 7 April 1939. No doubt Mussolini wanted to balance Hitler's successes with some of his own. As a result, President Franklin D. Roosevelt of the USA wrote to Hitler, asking him to promise not to invade any of the thirty countries listed in the letter.

While he was preparing his reply, Hitler celebrated his 50th birthday. The highlight was a huge military display and march-past in Berlin. Tanks rumbled through the streets, fighters and bombers roared overhead. The large group of foreign guests was very impressed.

Hitler's reply   On 28 April, Hitler delivered his reply to Roosevelt in a speech to the Reichstag broadcast round the world. It was a detailed explanation of his actions since 1933. Then he came to the question of Britain and Poland. As a result of their own treaty, he said, the German treaties with these two countries were no longer valid. Hitler therefore was ending the 1935 Anglo-German naval treaty and the 1934 Non-Aggression Treaty with Poland. In the second part of his speech, Hitler gave a long, mocking answer to Roosevelt. He made sarcastic remarks about the size of the USA compared with Germany. However, he failed to answer the one question — would he invade Poland?

Stalin and Hitler

Stalin's difficulties   Stalin had read the Russian translation of *Mein Kampf*. He knew of Hitler's goal to expand and take living space for Germany in the east which would include parts of the USSR. Yet the USSR was still struggling to industrialise and could not hope in the 1930s to check an all-out German advance. Stalin also feared widespread disloyalty among the Soviet peoples and in 1936–38 carried out a massive purge leading to the execution or imprisonment of hundreds of thousands. Among those executed were 80 per cent of all colonels or above in rank.

At least for the time being, Stalin had to find another way to resist Hitler's ambitions. One was to join with Britain and France in standing up to aggression. But this was unlikely to lead to an alliance with the Western powers because of their deep hostility to communism. On the other hand, the threat of an Anglo-French-Russian alliance might force Hitler to see the threat of being encircled. In that case he might be prepared to make an alliance with Stalin.

Stalin and Munich   The Munich agreement in September 1938 convinced Stalin that Britain and France had no real intentions of standing up to Hitler. He believed, on the contrary, that they were trying to point Hitler eastwards towards the communist USSR. That was probably not their intention but Hitler certainly saw Munich as opening the way for aggression in the east.

Wooing the French   Hitler may have believed that the Soviet army could be defeated easily, or simply that it would not aid the Poles if he attacked them. Certainly, Poland would have to be conquered before any attack on the Soviet Union. Yet he knew the Poles would resist and would call on their old ally, France. So Hitler needed to neutralise France while the goodwill of the Munich agreement lasted. On 6 December 1938 he persuaded the French to sign a join declaration that the French-German frontier would never be changed. Hitler gave up the German claim to Alsace-Lorraine in return, he hoped, for the French standing by while he moved against Poland.

That plan came to nothing when France joined Britain in guaranteeing Poland in March 1939. A few days later, on 3 April, Hitler issued his war plan against Poland. Then he turned to Italy and pressed Mussolini to sign a formal ten-year military and political alliance, the Pact of Steel of 22 May 1939.

Stalin and the West

Stalin could see clearly that Hitler's next move would be against Poland. Yet there was still the question of whether to link with Britain and France or to make a deal with Hitler. Shortly after their guarantees to Poland, the two powers had opened military talks with the USSR but there was an atmosphere of distrust. Stalin believed that the Western powers would be happy to see Germany and the USSR fight each other. Britain and France believed that Stalin's main aim was to extend Soviet rule over eastern Europe. It was always likely that the talks would break down and Stalin had another reason for preferring a pact with Germany. In 1938 fighting had broken out between the Japanese and forces of the Soviet Union with her allies in Mongolia. The last thing Stalin wanted was a two-front war against Japan and Germany.

Molotov

On 3 May, Stalin sent a very clear signal to Hitler. He dismissed his foreign minister, Maxim Litvinov, who favoured an alliance with Britain and France. Litvinov was also a Jew. V. M. Molotov was appointed in his place. The Germans saw the significance of this. Hitler, like Stalin, did not want a two-front war but he was determined to carry on and crush Poland. He planned an agreement to do this jointly with Stalin. In mid-June German-Soviet talks began.

Despite these talks, Stalin kept open the possibility of an alliance with the Western powers. On 22 July he invited Britain and France to send their military chiefs to Moscow for talks. They accepted but sent their men by sea so they did not arrive until 11 August. The Russian suspicion that Britain and France were not eager grew when it became clear that the military experts had been given very limited powers by their governments to make agreements.

Germany favoured

Hitler meanwhile had set 26 August as the date for his attack on Poland. He was very anxious to get a pact signed with the USSR. Stalin had now decided in favour of Germany. The talks with the British and French were suspended indefinitely on 21 August. Meanwhile German and Soviet officials were meeting and phone calls and telegrams passed between Moscow and Berlin.

Non-Aggression Treaty

On 23 August the German Foreign Minister Ribbentrop arrived in Moscow. The following day, in the early hours, he and Molotov signed a ten-year Non-Aggression Treaty. In addition, unknown until 1946, a secret section was added. This stated that if Germany did act against Poland, then eastern Poland, Finland, Latvia and Estonia would be left in the USSR's sphere of interest (i.e. to be taken over).

The British government immediately told Germany that they would stand by the Polish people if they were attacked. Two days later the British and Poles finally signed their Treaty, agreed in April. Hitler was also annoyed to learn that Italy was 'not ready' to go to war. He therefore postponed the attack on Poland until 1 September 1939. Last-minute attempts failed to persuade Britain not to get involved.

Half an hour after midday on 31 August 1939, Hitler issued orders to his army. The attack on Poland was to begin at 4.45 a.m. the following morning.

A British reporter wrote from Berlin on the very eve of war:

'At a quarter to one, exactly seventeen hours before German troops began their attack on Poland, Jane Leslie and I landed at the Tempelhof aerodrome in Berlin. From the moment we saw the grim rows of fighter planes lined up in the field – planes painted black with white swastikas – we felt the full drama of the awful moment. The capital was an armed camp. All private cars had been requisitioned and the only traffic in the streets was a stream of military lorries, armoured trucks and gun carriages that rumbled and clattered over the stone surfaces, terrible harbingers of the things to come. The hotels were crowded with the black uniforms of the Nazi storm troopers, and that night, for the first time, men were silhouetted against the sky, manning the anti-aircraft guns on the roof-tops along the Unter den Linden.

Everywhere you felt the sinister force of the German nation on the eve of launching its fifth war on Europe within the space of seventy-five years. . . .

You knew the machine was ready. This was the moment that Nazi Germany had worked for for six years. Now the planes and tanks were waiting and the guns were in position. Everything had been completed down to the polish on the last button of the last uniform. All that remained was for the lever to be pulled.'

Virginia Cowles, *Looking for Trouble*, 1941.

The Second World War

The invasion of Poland

Hitler drove through the almost empty streets of Berlin on 1 September to address the Reichstag. He did his best to put the blame on the Poles and denied any quarrel with Britain and France. He said he was ready to suffer the same hardships as the German people. If he were killed, Göring would succeed him.

Meanwhile two army groups were attacking Poland. One operated out of northern Germany (including East Prussia) and one from

Czechoslovakia and Silesia. The Germans and the Poles each had well over 1 million soldiers. The Germans, however, had 3600 armoured vehicles and 1900 aircraft. The Poles had only 750 such vehicles and 900 aircraft. Where the Poles outnumbered the Germans eleven to one was in cavalry!

Britain and France declare war

On 1 September, Hitler had agreed to Mussolini's request that Italy remain neutral. Britain and France gave Hitler until 11 a.m. on Sunday 3 September to withdraw all his forces from Poland. Hitler failed to do this and so after twenty-five years and one month, Europe went to war again.

Poland defeated

The outdated Polish army was no match for the Germans. The Polish airforce was destroyed on the ground or shot down. The powerful *panzer* (armoured) divisions, supported by Stuka dive-bombers, tore through the Polish defences. Warsaw and other cities were heavily bombed.

Soviet invasion

Stalin now took a hand in accordance with the secret part of the Nazi-Soviet Pact. On 17 September, Soviet troops entered eastern Poland and ended any hope the Poles might have had of resistance. Warsaw was captured ten days later. All fighting ended on 6 October. Meanwhile, Ribbentrop and Molotov had signed a new treaty sharing out Poland. Hitler got most of Poland. In return, Lithuania, the Baltic State went to Stalin.

Polish losses

Over 100,000 Polish people were killed compared with 11,000 Germans and 700 Russians. A million Poles were captured. One-fifth that number fled abroad to fight again. Only in aircraft (560–330) were German losses higher than the Poles'.

Hitler's Propaganda Minister, Dr Joseph Goebbels wrote in his diary, 2 November 1939, describing Warsaw:

'Warsaw: this is Hell. A city reduced to ruins. Our bombs and shells have done a thorough job. No house is undamaged. The populace is apathetic, shadowy. The people creep through the streets like insects. It is repulsive and scarcely describable.

Up on the citadel. Here everything has been destroyed. Hardly a stone left standing. Here Polish nationalism went through its years of suffering. We must eliminate it utterly, or one day it will rise again.'

Ed. Fred Taylor, *The Goebbels Diaries 1939–1941*, 1983.

The 'Phoney' War

Inaction in the West

Despite desperate appeals from Poland, British and French forces made no move to attack Germany. This convinced Hitler that the Western powers were hopelessly weak. After the collapse of Poland, he made

Two years after the fall of Poland, Polish Jewish children are rounded up in Warsaw by German soldiers

a new peace offer to Britain and France. All they needed to do was to give him total freedom in eastern Europe. Both refused it.

Hitler then ordered an immediate attack on the West. The military chiefs managed to convince him this was not possible, especially as winter was approaching. Reluctantly, Hitler postponed the attack until the summer of 1940. The lack of action on the western front created the term 'Phoney War'.

USSR and Finland   On 30 November the USSR attacked Finland, after she had refused to hand over territory near to Leningrad which Stalin wanted to make his country's defences more secure. Hitler was furious at the Soviet action and so was Mussolini.

The Soviet attack was at first a total failure. Finnish ski-troops inflicted heavy casualties on the untrained Soviet forces. Massed attacks by large Soviet forces were driven back. Eventually with an army of twenty-seven divisions, the USSR cracked the Finnish resistance. The Finns were forced to hand over important parts of their country. The USSR lost 100,000 dead but it had given notice to Hitler that Stalin would be ruthless in defending Soviet territory.

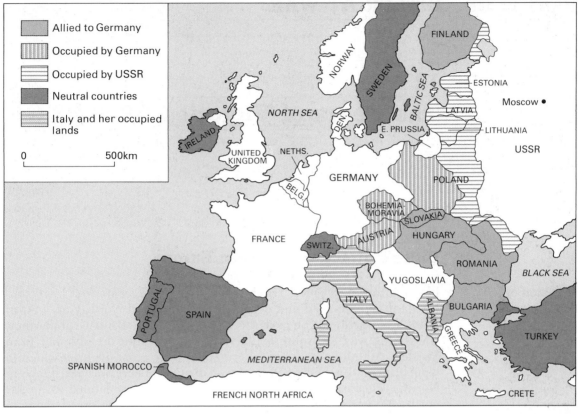

Legend

	Allied to Germany
	Occupied by Germany
	Occupied by USSR
	Neutral countries
	Italy and her occupied lands

0   500km

Changes in Eastern Europe, 1939–40

Goebbels in the West

Meanwhile, the German generals continued to plan the defeat of the Western allies. Dr Goebbels, Hitler's Propaganda Minister, wrote in his diary following a visit to the western front during the Phoney War:

'8 December 1939 (Friday)
From Aachen along the Belgian and Luxembourg borders. On the way we view fantastic new fortifications, some still under construction.

During the journey I get out of the car frequently and talk to the soldiers and the construction workers. There are some difficulties everywhere. But the morale is excellent. My mind is set fully at rest.

Short stop in Prum. Then it's straight on to the French front. Through totally ruined villages which had been in French possession and were deserted by the civilian population. Only soldiers to be seen. A striking impression.

One becomes totally convinced that no one will break through here.

Drive to the foremost positions. A general and a colonel are waiting for us. We wade through deep muck and dirt. One can see the French lying there on the other side.

Ed. Fred Taylor, *The Goebbels Diaries 1939–1941*, 1983.

12
The Years of Victories, 1940–42

Hitler's attack on western Europe

Invasion of Scandinavia

Before attacking France, Hitler decided he must secure first his northern flank. He invaded and occupied Denmark and Norway on 7 April 1940. This action protected the Baltic Sea from British submarines. The Baltic was the route for Germany's vital iron ore supplies from Sweden. Additionally, it gave Germany a huge coastline from which to launch air and submarine attacks on Britain. There was resistance in Norway where 20,000 British and allied troops were landed in the far north, but eventually Germany's superior air power forced them to retreat.

By the time Norway was totally occupied, 140 German divisions were ready for action in western Europe. Opposing them were 104 French, 10 British, 22 Belgian and 8 Dutch divisions. With over 3000 tanks, the French outnumbered Germany's 2445. However, Germany's air force of 5446 planes vastly outnumbered the Allies' 3099.

Dunkirk

The German attack began on 10 May 1940. The Allies were caught by surprise. Chamberlain resigned and Winston Churchill succeeded him as Prime Minister. The German forces broke through the Allied lines. The Netherlands was bombed into defeat. Within ten days almost 400,000 Allied troops were trapped along the French and Belgian coasts. Between 27 May and 4 June, 338,000 men were rescued from the beaches and harbour at Dunkirk. Warships, merchant ships and a fleet of 900 small boats joined in the rescue.

Armistice

On 5 June, the German army turned on the remaining sixty-five French divisions along a 650-kilometre front. Five days later Mussolini declared war on France. On 14 June the Germans entered Paris. Two days later, the French government asked for an armistice. This was signed on the 22nd at Compiègne, where the Germans had surrendered in 1918.

Hitler's total victory had cost the lives of 'only' 27,000 Germans.

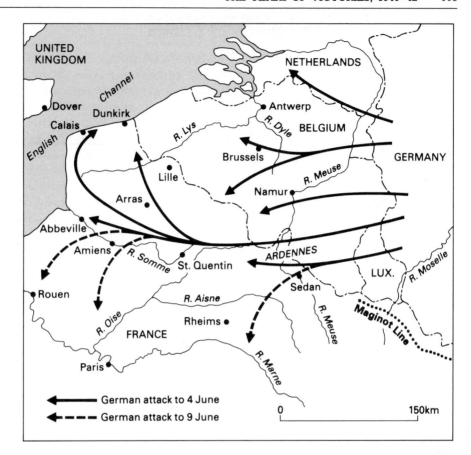

The conquest of North-West Europe

German infantry resting in a French village, June 1940

The Battle of Britain

Peace feelers

Hitler hoped that Britain would accept German rule over Europe and give up the fight. He made some concessions to tempt her. First, he ordered the occupation only of northern France. The south was left under the Vichy government of Marshal Petain, France's First World War hero. He also left the French fleet disarmed, at anchor. Churchill, however, made it clear that there would be 'no deals'. In a speech on 16 July, President Roosevelt gave strong backing to Churchill. Hitler ordered his generals to begin planning the invasion of Britain.

Operation 'Sea Lion'

The plan, code-named 'Sea Lion', was ready on 13 July. There were many difficult problems. The Royal Navy controlled the Channel. Without command of the sea, the German invasion fleet and supply vessels would be sunk. Only if the Germans controlled the air also could the Royal Navy be driven away. Hitler clearly was neither enthusiastic nor optimistic. On 29 July 1940 he issued another order to the army: to prepare for the invasion of the USSR in May 1941!

'Destroy the RAF'

Hitler decided an all-out air attack on southern England was the only hope for launching a successful invasion. On 13 August 'Operation Eagle' began. Britain was well-prepared. Although outnumbered in planes, the Spitfire and Hurricane fighters were outstanding. Radar enabled the squadrons to be assembled in the right place at the right time. Even more important, the British had *Ultra*, the key to Germany's top-secret codes. Almost every German radio message could be intercepted and translated at *Ultra* headquarters at Bletchley in Oxfordshire. This closely-guarded secret gave the Allied leaders an enormous advantage throughout the war.

As the Luftwaffe continued its attacks, so its losses grew, at two to three times the rate of the British. By the end of August 1940 the *Luftwaffe* was bombing London and the RAF Berlin.

Sea Lion postponed

By mid-September, Hitler admitted defeat. The *Luftwaffe*, rather than the RAF, was being destroyed and the bombing campaign was not forcing Britain to surrender. On 17 September 'Sea Lion' was postponed.

The RAF and the *Luftwaffe* continued to attack each other's major cities. Exeter, Southampton, Bristol, Coventry, Liverpool, Sheffield, Hull, Clydebank, and even Belfast, all suffered. London, however, remained the principal target in Britain, while it was the industrial towns in western Germany that suffered most on the other side.

The invasion of the USSR

Operation Barbarossa

On 18 December 1940, Hitler issued his final orders to prepare plans for the invasion of the USSR. The date was to be 15 May 1941 and the attack was code-named 'Barbarossa'. It was to consist of three great thrusts; aimed at Leningrad, Moscow, and the Crimea.

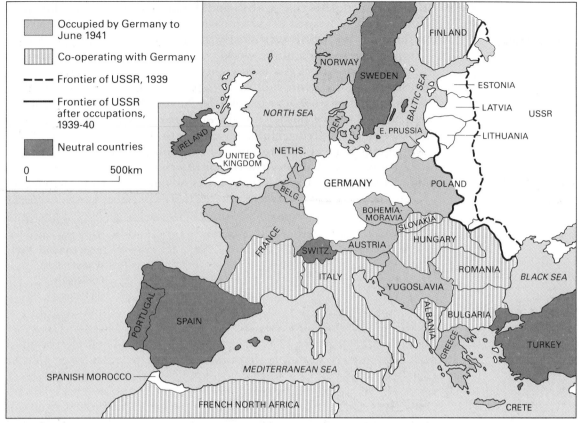

German gains by June 1941

Mussolini in trouble

Mussolini, ignored by Hitler, determined to show that he too was an independent military leader. In October 1940, using Albania as a base, he invaded Greece. That campaign was a disaster and the Italians were driven back. Britain sent an army to help the Greeks and on 11 November, British bombers crippled the Italian fleet lying in harbour at Taranto. From December 1940 to February 1941, British forces in North Africa drove back the Italians. 113,000 Italians were captured. Britain lost only 438 killed in her first major ground victory of the war.

Yugoslavia

Greece was not Hitler's only worry in south-east Europe. In March 1941 Prince Paul of Yugoslavia, who supported Hitler, was overthrown by a revolution. Hitler was furious. German and Hungarian troops attacked Yugoslavia savagely. It was forced to surrender in eleven days. Greece now lay open to German invasion. Despite being reinforced by 60,000 British troops, the country fell in fifteen days.

Warnings to Stalin

The war in the Balkans forced Hitler to postpone 'Barbarossa' for six weeks. Stalin was determined to try to keep on good terms with Hitler and continued to deliver raw materials to Germany punctually, ignoring German aircraft violations of Soviet airspace.

On 13 April 1941 the USSR and Japan signed a neutrality pact. Neither country wanted a war in eastern Siberia. Despite this success, the threat to the USSR was clearly growing.

From different parts of the world, warnings poured in that Germany was planning to attack. At least eighty distinct warnings were received but Stalin ignored them all. He believed that they were planted by British intelligence services to split the Nazi-Soviet Pact. The orders to Soviet troops on the border remained the same. There must be no risk of a border clash giving Hitler an excuse to invade.

Hitler did not need an excuse. The German attack began at dawn on 22 June, 1941. The result was a disaster for the Soviet forces on the border. On the first day, German tanks advanced up to 60 kilometres.

Operation Barbarossa — the attack on the Soviet Union

1200 Soviet planes were destroyed, many on the ground; railways, oil and ammunition dumps were all devastated.

4 million men

For the attack on the USSR, Hitler had assembled the most powerful force in history. It consisted of ten armies from all parts of Fascist Europe, but was almost 75 per cent German. 4.6 million men and 5000 aircraft, 3700 tanks and 50,000 heavy guns and mortars were used. The USSR had almost 3 million men facing their attackers, but only 1800 modern tanks and 1500 modern aircraft.

Leningrad and Moscow

The Germans continued to advance quickly, killing and capturing hundreds of thousands of Soviet troops. In August they surrounded the USSR's second city, Leningrad. Rather than slow down their march across the Soviet Union, they left a force to besiege the city. At the time no-one knew that the siege would last for thirty months.

On 30 September General von Bock began his drive on Moscow with 1 million men, 1700 tanks and 950 aircraft. His forces broke the main Red Army resistance but, as they neared the city, they lost momentum. The weather was appalling; first mud, then bitter cold. 30 kilometres from the Soviet capital they came to a halt, exhausted and freezing.

Zhukov's counter-attack

Stalin ordered General Georgi Zhukov, victor over the Japanese in 1939, to take charge of the defence of Moscow. With no fear of a Japanese attack in eastern Siberia, Zhukov brought up large forces of Siberian troops used to the cold. On 5 December 1941, Zhukov counter-attacked the Germans in front of Moscow. Soon the Germans were retreating up to 250 kilometres and on 8 December the German Army was ordered on to the defensive. Hitler took personal command.

Their first Russian winter was a bitter experience for German troops

World-wide war

Pearl Harbor

On 7 December, Japanese planes had attacked the US Pacific Fleet at Pearl Harbor, in Hawaii. Four days later Germany declared war on the USA. The Soviet-Japanese neutrality pact survived. Six months earlier Hitler had been in a position of almost total control over Europe, except for Britain, the neutrals and the USSR. By the end of 1941 his invincible army was spreadeagled across the frozen Russian landscape. Moreover, he now faced the formidable alliance of the USA, the USSR and Britain and her Empire. This alliance had an industrial production more than three times larger than Germany and its allies, and more than twice the population.

Soviet failures

By February 1942 the Soviet counter-offensive had come to an exhausted halt. Hundreds of thousands of Soviet troops died in badly planned attacks. These were mainly in the Crimea, the Ukraine and, unsuccessfully, trying to end the German seige of Leningrad. More than 1.1 million Germans had been killed, wounded, frostbitten or captured since 22 June 1941. Soviet losses were several times higher than this.

Rommel in North Africa

In April 1941, Hitler had sent General Erwin Rommel and the Afrika Korps to reinforce the Italians in North Africa. With only three divisions and the unreliable Italians in support, Rommel attacked. He reached the Egyptian frontier and laid siege to Tobruk. Fortunately for the Allies, he had neither the men nor the supplies to get further.

British counter-attack

In November 1941, the British hit back. Rommel was pushed back and Tobruk was relieved after nine months. In 1942 it was Rommel's turn to attack although he was still short of supplies through shipping losses in the Mediterranean. Late in May 1942 his forces swept back into Egypt. They were finally halted at El Alamein (see page 135).

The Battle of Stalingrad

1942 offensive

By the summer of 1942, Hitler had managed to find replacements for about half of his losses on the eastern front. However, they were mostly from his 'allies', Romania, Hungary, Italy, Slovakia and even one division of Spanish volunteers. The total number of men, about 5 million on each side, was about equal. The USSR had the advantage in tanks.

Hitler's plan for 1942 was to capture the Caspian oilfields. Hitler also had a fantasy of his forces continuing into the Middle East. There they would link up with Rommel coming north out of Egypt. Then this joint German army would move east into Persia (Iran). There it would eventually link up with the Japanese after the latter's planned conquest of India. Such were Hitler's daydreams in 1942.

Stalingrad

Hitler could not fail to be attracted to the idea of capturing the 'city

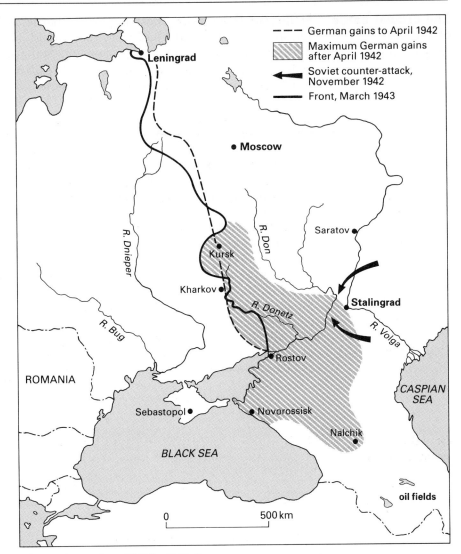

War in the southern USSR, 1942–3

of Stalin' also. The generals told him the armies in the south were not strong enough to capture both the oil fields and Stalingrad. At that point, the 6th Army was moving on Stalingrad and the 4th Panzer Army was poised to attack either target.

Hitler used the 4th Panzer Army for both goals but in the wrong order. He sent it south towards the oilfields where it was not needed. Then he sent it back to Stalingrad by which time the Soviet army had got just enough reinforcements in to hold the city.

The 4th Panzer and 6th Armies became trapped in an enormous street-by-street battle in Stalingrad. Meanwhile, further south, the advance on the oilfields came to a halt. Had the 4th Panzer attacked Stalingrad two weeks sooner, it might have captured the city. Then it could have handed over to the 6th and gone south to the oilfields.

The crucial battle of the war

Stalingrad became the most important battle of World War Two in Europe. If the Germans had won, they would have been able to swing north up the Volga to take Moscow and Stalin might have had to accept a humiliating peace. Britain and the USA would then have had to decide whether to continue the war alone.

Hitler's war at sea

U-boats

The war at sea followed a similar pattern to 1914–18. Britain's huge surface fleet was able to blockade Germany and its allies and prevent food and raw materials getting in. The main threat to Britain came from Germany's submarines (U-boats). On 3 September 1939 the liner *Athenia*, carrying 1400 passengers, was torpedoed in the Atlantic. Within three months German U-boats were attacking allied shipping without warning.

Twenty a week

By 1942 the U-boats were sinking twenty allied cargo ships each week. Simultaneously, allied counter measures were improving. These included special 'sounding' devices for 'spotting' submerged U-boats and specially designed hunter aircraft. By 1943 the wolfpacks of U-boats were being hunted down. By the end of the war, out of a total of 1162 U-boats, the allies had sunk almost 800.

13
Germany and Europe under Nazi Rule, 1939–45

The German economy at war

Pre-war strains

During 1933–39 the main feature of the German economy had concerned re-armament. The army had increased from 7 to 103 divisions. The *Luftwaffe* had not existed in 1933. By 1939 it had 4000 front-line aircraft. The navy had also grown rapidly even though it took longer to build battle cruisers than fighter planes. All this led to massive spending and serious shortages of raw materials and skilled labour.

War for profit

The strain of re-armament meant that in 1939 Germany had some serious weaknesses. She was not prepared for a long war against an alliance of strong powers. Germany had prepared for short *blitzkreig* (lightning) wars or unopposed occupations against smaller opponents. These adventures were profitable; the occupation of Austria produced $200 million in gold and foreign currency. The conquest of France provided large quantities of food and other payments for Germany.

This table illustrates the economic exploitation of conquered countries by the German occupying forces:

Payments of occupation costs in billions of Reichmarks (Rm)

Country	1940 (2nd half)	1941	1942	1943	1944 (till Sept)	Total
France	1.75	5.55	8.55	11.10	8.30	35.25
Holland	0.80	1.90	2.20	2.20	1.65	8.75
Belgium	0.35	1.30	1.50	1.60	0.95	5.70
Denmark	0.20	0.20	0.25	0.55	0.80	2.00
Italy				2.00	8.00	10.00
Others	0.90	1.05	4.50	7.55	8.30	22.30
Total	4.00	10.00	17.00	25.00	28.00	84.00

1-RM in 1940 = £1 in 1990 prices.

Help from the East

The supply of raw materials from the East was even more important. Oil from Romania came up the Danube in barges. There was plunder from Poland. Stalin, frightened by Germany's 'invincible' army, sent increased supplies of vital raw materials in an attempt to buy off Hitler.

Total war

The tactics which defeated Poland and France did not work against the USSR. By December 1941, despite massive advances and victories, the USSR was far from being defeated. With the USA involved against it as well, Germany had to prepare for 'total war'.

Fritz Todt

The man who planned Germany's 'total war' economy was Fritz Todt. He was a civil engineer who had been in charge of the *autobahnen* (motorways) and Westwall construction in the 1930s. On 17 March 1940, Hitler appointed him Minister of Armaments and Munitions. At first he had limited powers. Many other people in Germany were involved in weapons production and did not want to give up their powers. However, Todt began re-organising production to increase the efficiency, quality and output of weapons and munitions. Hitler supported him as losses in the USSR increased. On 10 January 1942, Hitler ordered massive increases in all types of ground and air weapons, and U-boats. A month later Todt was killed in an air crash.

Albert Speer

Speer was Hitler's architect. Two hours after learning of Todt's death, Hitler told him to take over as Minister. Speer was skilful and strong-minded enough to get his way. He asked for and received the extra powers needed to increase production of weapons.

German armament production grew rapidly under Speer's direction. For every 100 tanks built when he took over in February 1942, almost 600 were built in December 1944. In July 1944 aircraft production was 367 and overall total armament production was 322; each compared with 100 in February 1942. In each case these were the highest figures ever achieved, and production then fell.

Central Planning Board

The secret of Speer's success was the Central Planning Board, established by Hitler on 4 April 1942. It consisted of three men including Speer. Within a month, Speer had complete control of the munitions industry. The Board controlled the allocation of raw materials. Thus, if Speer wished to increase tank production, he sent more steel to the tank factories. If he wished to reduce warship production he sent less steel to the shipyards. It was a simple but effective method.

Labour

It was also important to control the labour force. On 31 July 1939 there were almost 10.5 million industrial workers in Germany. Of these, more than 2.5 million were women. As the war continued, more men were called into the armed forces. By April 1943 the industrial labour force had fallen below 8 million. The number of women workers, however, scarcely changed throughout the war. Hitler believed that a 'woman's place is in the home'. Unlike Britain where women were conscripted, Germany did not use this source of labour.

Foreign workers   Germany tried to fill the labour gap with foreigners. Both civilians and prisoners of war (POWs) were used. The total rose from 1.15 million in 1940 to 4.1 million in 1942 and over 7 million in 1944. Of the last figure, 1.8 million were POWs. Thus, by the summer of 1944, the number of foreign workers in Germany (7.1 million) almost equalled the total number of German industrial workers (7.5 million). The largest supply of foreign labour came from the USSR.

Slave labour   Very few foreign workers came voluntarily. Most were rounded up at gunpoint and became slave labour. Even ten- to fourteen-year-olds were seized and sent to Germany in freight wagons. Conditions were appalling. The slave labourers worked in factories for long hours and almost no pay. They lived in overcrowded, unheated camps with poor food and clothing and no medical attention. They died by the thousands. The fortunate ones were those sent to work on German farms; conditions were better there. Obviously the efficiency of slave labour was much less than that of Germany's workers. It was the first reason for the eventual collapse of the economy.

Collapse   After reaching its highest production in the second half of 1944, the German munitions industry quickly collapsed. The second reason, after manpower problems, was the allied bombing campaign. About 80 per cent of all the bombing raids on Germany were in 1944–45. The *Luftwaffe* was unable to prevent Allied bombing raids. Attacks on Germany's railways, particularly in the Ruhr, were very damaging. In the early years of the war, 22,000 wagons of coal had moved out from there each day. By November 1944 bombing had reduced this to 5000 wagons. Bombing raids on refineries cut back German production of aircraft fuel and weakened air defences still further.

Another major cause of economic collapse was the reconquest of territories by the Allies. For example, on 29 August 1944 the Soviet Army captured Germany's main oil source, the Ploesti oilfields in Romania. Neutral countries such as Sweden and Turkey also reduced exports of vital materials as Germany's defeat approached. When Soviet troops took Silesia and Anglo-American forces seized the Ruhr in the spring of 1945, Germany's war production machine was finally destroyed.

The euthanasia programme

'Racial cleansing'   Hitler believed that the Germans were a race of supermen. He despised people of 'inferior' races such as the Slavs (who included the Russians and many other peoples of eastern Europe) and especially Jews. He also wanted to increase Germany's strength by 'racial cleansing'. This meant destroying what were considered to be worthless lives: the mentally ill and the handicapped. This programme, which began early in 1939, is usually called the 'euthanasia programme'. Today euthanasia refers to the 'mercy killing' at their own request of people suffering serious illnesses from which they will not recover.

Child killing

The programme was organised by the Reich Committee under Phillip Boulher. Handicapped children were the first to be killed. The programme was kept secret; the methods used were starvation or a deadly injection. Over 5000 were killed in this way.

The murder of handicapped children at a clinic near Munich in 1940 was described by a witness:

'About forty visitors in uniforms of the most varied hues, from the dark grey of the Wehrmacht via the bright brown of the cadre officials of the Nazi Party to the jet black of the SS, gathered round Dr Pfannmuller.

After some brief introductory remarks, Dr Pfannmuller approached one of the fifteen cots which flanked the central passage to the right and left.

"We have here children aged from one to five", he pontificated. "All these creatures represent for me as a National Socialist 'living burdens' . . . a burden for our nation . . . In this sense, the Führer's action to free the national community from this overburdening is quite simply a national deed, whose greatness non-medical men will only be able to assess after a period of years if not decades. We do not carry out the action with poison, injections or other measures which can be recognised . . . for then the foreign press and certain circles in Paris or London would only have new opportunities for propaganda against us . . . No, our method is much simpler".

With these words he pulled a child out of its cot. While this fat, gross man displayed the whimpering skeletal little person like a hare which he had just caught, he coolly remarked: "Naturally we don't stop their food straight away. That would cause too much fuss. We gradually reduce their portions. Nature then takes care of the rest . . . This one won't last more than two or three more days."'

The adult programme

The killing of adults was also organised in 1939. Boulher was again put in charge. He was assisted by four psychiatrists. All asylums and clinics were required to register severely handicapped, mentally ill and helpless patients. War-wounded were excluded. The key decision was whether a patient could work. If not, they were likely to be killed. In Hitler's mind it was not simply a question of destroying a 'worthless life'; he was also releasing the nursing staff for more 'profitable' work such as caring for wounded soldiers. It was estimated that there were a maximum of 75,000 'worthless lives' to be ended.

Gassing

The first patients were killed by injections but this was found to be 'too slow'. An experimental gas chamber was built at Brandenburg Asylum, Berlin, in January 1940. The bodies were cremated immediately. Even before this the SS had begun shooting thousands of Polish mentally ill patients in the autumn of 1939. The gas chambers proved to be the most effective way of killing large numbers of people. About 20,000 patients were gassed and then cremated at Hartsheim extermination centre, near Linz in Austria.

Letters were sent to the relations of the handicapped and mentally ill who had been murdered. They were told that their loved ones had died of pneumonia or another infectious disease. Naturally many mistakes were made. One patient who had his appendix removed in 1930 was supposed to have died of appendicitis!

Growing protests

News soon began to get out about the gassings. The groups most concerned were the judiciary (judges and lawyers) and the church. Only one judge, Lothar Kreyssig, had the courage to complain. So did Pastor Braune, Vice President of the Protestant welfare organisation – he was arrested by the Gestapo. The Roman Catholic Church's bishops protested at their conference in August 1940. A few months later the Pope, Pius XII, issued a statement condemning euthanasia. However, it was nearly a year (3 August 1941) later that the Archbishop of Munster, Clemens von Galen, preached a long sermon attacking the whole programme. The sermon was printed and widely distributed and further protests followed. On 24 August 1941 Hitler stopped the programme after a total of 71,088 persons had been murdered in this way.

A German worker employed to cremate the victims of gassing described his work:

'Once the room had been aired, we burners – we always had twelve hour shifts – had to get the corpses out of the gas chamber and bring them into the mortuary. The mortuary was next to the gas canister room. Getting the corpses out of the gas chamber into the mortuary was a difficult and nerve-racking task. It was not easy to disentangle the corpses which were locked together and drag them into the mortuary. This task was made even more difficult initially by the fact that the floor was uneven and when the floor was concreted it was rough. This made dragging the corpses into the mortuary difficult. Later, when the floor was tiled we put water down. That made moving the dead much easier. The corpses were piled up in the mortuary. Next to the mortuary was the crematorium. The crematorium was equipped with a so-called pan which could be taken out of the oven. The dead were laid on this pan and were pushed in and left there just like a baking oven. Depending on the number of corpses, we burnt 2–8 at a time. The oven was coke-fired. The work went on night and day as required. Before the corpses were burnt the burners pulled out the gold teeth of those who had been marked with a cross.

Since the work was very exhausting and, as I said, nerve-racking, we got about $\frac{1}{4}$ liter of schnaps per day. I reckon that we burnt about 20,000 mentally ill people in this way.

Hitler's war on the Jews

In September 1939 about 250,000 out of Germany's original 550,000 Jewish people had not left the country or already been murdered. In

Poland, by contrast, there were more than 3.1 million Jews. Of these 1.9 million were living under German occupation. The Nazis immediately began a campaign of terror, humiliation and restrictions on Poland's Jews such as a curfew between 9 p.m. and 5 a.m.

Deportations

The top Nazis had still not decided finally in 1940 how to deal with the Jewish populations of Poland and other countries ruled by Germany. At first they thought about creating a large Jewish reservation near Lublin in Poland. This had been tried but was abandoned after a few months. It caused too much disruption.

Forced labour

The next stage was to turn the Jews into forced slave labour. Digging ditches and roadmaking were typical of the work done. The hours were long and back-breaking, housing and food were awful and even the sick had to work. The death rate was very high.

Ghettoes

In September 1940, Heydrich ordered that all Polish Jews should be placed in ghettoes in cities. This meant that a part of the city would be walled off. The Jews would be kept inside like a prison. Lodz, with more than 300,000 Jews, was the first city chosen. All fit persons in the Lodz ghetto worked as slave labourers.

The Warsaw ghetto was even larger; about 560,000 Jews lived there. There was terrible overcrowding and most houses were unheated in winter. Food supplies were totally inadequate. Each person in the ghetto received about one-eighth of the amount needed to preserve health. Diseases were widespread and the average death toll was more than 4000 per month. Even in these terrible conditions, the Jews ran schools and held religious services.

German Jews

Further restrictions were placed on German Jews in late 1939. They were forbidden to own radios or buy cakes or chocolates. They were not given clothing coupons or allowed to go into shops except between 4 p.m. and 5 p.m. German Jews were encouraged to emigrate. One wild plan was to send all Jews to Madagascar, a French colony.

The Einsatzgruppen

The invasion of the Soviet Union in June 1941 sealed the fate of Europe's Jews. Hitler believed that Jews and communists were almost one and the same. Now he could begin to exterminate both. For this purpose four *Einsatzgruppen* (Special Units) were formed, consisting of 600–1000 men each. They were mostly recruited from the SS and various police units such as the Gestapo.

The *Einsatzgruppen* were spread out behind the invading armies. Their orders were simple: to execute Communist Party officials, saboteurs, resistance fighters and Jews. The *Einsatzgruppen* began shooting all these people when captured. They killed all captured Jews, men, women and children. They also killed several thousand gypsies.

According to their own claims, the *Einsatzgruppen* murdered more than 700,000 persons, mostly Jews in the USSR, up to April 1942. These included German, Austrian and Czech Jews deported to Poland.

Hermann Graebe, a German engineer, witnessed the slaughter of Jews in Dubno, USSR, by the *Einsatzgruppen*:

'I walked round the mound and stood in front of the huge grave. The bodies were lying so tightly packed together that only their heads showed, from almost all of which blood ran down over their shoulders. Some were still moving. Others raised their hands and turned their heads to show they were still alive. The ditch was already three quarters full. I estimate that it already held about a thousand bodies. I turned my eyes towards the man doing the shooting. He was an SS man; he sat, legs swinging, on the edge of the ditch. He had an automatic rifle resting on his knees and was smoking a cigarette. The people, completely naked, climbed down steps which had been cut into the clay wall of the ditch, stumbled over the heads of those lying there and stopped at the spot indicated by the SS man. They lay down on top of the dead or wounded; some stroked those still living and spoke quietly to them. Then I heard a series of rifle shots. I looked into the ditch and saw the bodies contorting or, the heads already inert, sinking on the corpses beneath. Blood flowed from the nape of their necks. I was surprised not to be ordered away, but I noticed three postmen in uniform standing nearby. Then the next batch came up, climbed down into the ditch, laid themselves next to the previous victim and were shot.'

The 'final solution'

The Wannsee Conference

By the summer of 1941 the leading Nazis and SS commanders were certain that Hitler wished to exterminate all Jews living in German-controlled countries. It was also clear that the mass killings could take place only in eastern Poland where they might be kept secret. It would be an enormous task to move up to 10 million people from different parts of Europe to eastern Poland. To discuss this horrific plan, Heydrich called a conference of fifteen people at Wannsee in Berlin for 20 January 1942.

The written account of the conference referred to the 'evacuation' of Jews to the east as the 'final solution'. Everyone knew this meant extermination.

Gas vans

The mass shootings of Jews was noisy, semi-public and required large amounts of alcohol for the gunmen before and after. After watching a mass shooting, Himmler decided that another method should be used. The first alternative was the use of fifteen gas vans. The gas was carbon monoxide transported in cylinders from Germany. The first gas vans were based at Chelmno from December 1941 to January 1943. During this period 145,000 gypsies, Poles and Russians, the last two mostly Jews, were murdered there.

The death camps

In the view of Nazi exterminators, the gas vans were proving too small and too few for the massive killings planned. They decided to build camps in Poland with large gas chambers. There would be crematoria also for burning the corpses. The first, at Belzec, began operations in March 1942. By December it had consumed 500,000 victims. The second camp, Sobibor, operated from April 1942 to October 1943. Up to 200,000 Jews died there. Treblinka camp also opened in April 1943 and was closed on 19 August after an uprising by prisoners.

Jewish children behind barbed wire in Auschwitz when the Red Army liberated the camp

Auschwitz

The largest and most infamous of the death camps was Auschwitz in southern Poland. It was planned as a concentration camp for Polish prisoners in May 1940. Rudolph Hoess was its commandant. An artificial rubber works was planned there using prisoners as labour. In 1941 Himmler told Hoess to adapt Auschwitz for large-scale extermination by gassing. The first killings, of Soviet prisoners of war, took place on 3 September 1941. Zyclon B, a gas used for pest control, was adapted for human use. It was easy to obtain and it killed quickly.

The first Jewish victims arrived at Auschwitz early in 1942. The camp was progressively extended until it covered 50 square kilometres. The last transport of Jewish prisoners arrived on 3 November 1944. On 27 January 1945 Soviet troops liberated the camp. According to Rudolf Hoess, approximately 1.1 million Jews were murdered at Auschwitz. The largest group was 400,000 Hungarians, all of whom arrived after March 1944. The next largest was 250,000 from Poland; 110,000 came from France and 100,000 from Germany.

The Holocaust

It is not possible to estimate accurately the total number of Jews murdered in the Holocaust. The highest estimate is about 5.7 million, the lowest 4.2 million. Whatever the final figure, it is known that 50 per cent of the total were Polish and about 16 per cent Soviet citizens. The remainder came mostly from central and south-eastern Europe. In western Europe only France and Holland lost very large numbers. Denmark lost 'only' 100 Jews.

Hitler had set out to destroy Germany's Jews and almost succeeded. When he came to power there were 550,000 German Jews. In 1989 there were about 27,000 of whom only 4500 were aged between sixteen and thirty. This is one human measure of the scale of the Holocaust itself, together with the flight of Jews from Germany before it began and the post-war emigration of those who survived the camps to build new lives in Israel and other countries such as the United States.

Rudolf Hoess, Commandant of Auschwitz, recorded the peak of mass killings in 1944:

> 'Auschwitz reached its high point in the spring of 1944. Long trains travelled backwards and forwards between the subsidiary camp of Birkenau and Hungary . . . A triple track railway line leading to the new crematoria enabled a train to be unloaded while the next one was arriving. The percentage of those who were assigned to 'special accommodation' – the term which had been used for some time in place of 'special treatment' – was particularly high in the case of these transports . . . All four crematoria operated at full blast. However, soon the ovens were burnt out as a result of the continuous heavy use and only crematorium No. 111 was still smoking . . . The special commandos had been increased and worked feverishly to keep emptying the gas chambers . . . The last body had hardly been pulled from the gas chambers and dragged across the yard behind the crematorium, which was covered in corpses, to the burning pit, when the next lot were already undressing in the hall ready for gassing.'

Europe's gypsies

Close to the Jews in the Nazis hate-list were Europe's 936,000 gypsies and travelling people. They were hunted down almost as ruthlessly as the Jews. They were shot, gassed, starved and given fatal injections. Because of their smaller numbers and isolated life-styles, they were easier to find and round up. The result was that in some countries, notably Holland, Luxembourg, Lithuania and Estonia, almost every gypsy was murdered. In Croatia (Yugoslavia) only 500 survived out of 28,500. In all approximately 220,000 gypsies (23.5 per cent) were murdered by Hitler's men.

14
Resistance

Resistance outside Germany

Civilians and POWs massacred

In the First World War, most of the 8.6 million deaths were among soldiers. In the Second World War, the deaths of civilians were at least equal to those of the military. The Soviet Union lost 7 million civilians, Poland 6 million, Germany 3.6 million and Yugoslavia 1.7 million. Civilians died in almost every way that soldiers, sailors and airmen did. Air-raids, starvation and the death camps killed more civilians than military. Overall the largest death tolls were in the countries of eastern Europe and the USSR. It was through these that Hitler's war machine rampaged most fiercely. There the SS had a totally free licence to kill. It was also there that the resistance movements were the largest, the best organised and the most troublesome to the Nazi occupiers.

Soviet resistance

When German forces first entered the Soviet Union in 1941, they were in many places greeted as liberators. This was because Stalin's reign of terror in the 1930s had antagonised so many people. This situation soon changed. Hitler regarded the Soviet people as sub-human. They were treated abominably. Those who were not shot, blown up or frozen to death were either sent to Germany as slave workers or left to starve. The result was that by 1943 up to 1 million Soviet partisans were operating behind the German lines. They attacked German bases, convoys and railways and killed large numbers of German soldiers. The Germans had to employ many divisions on anti-partisan duties, which reduced the number of men available at the front.

Soviet POWs

During the first six months of the war against the USSR, the Germans captured over 3.5 million Soviet troops. These POWs were surrounded by barbed wire and left to starve without shelter or help of any kind. Only when Hitler realised the war was going to be a lengthy struggle did he allow Soviet POWs to be kept alive as slave labour. Many thousands were recruited into the German army as an alternative to being left to starve. Those who survived were mostly forcibly sent back to the USSR in 1945.

British and American POWs were treated much less harshly than Soviet ones. There were, however, several massacres of western prisoners during the War.

Poland

Despite their rapid defeat in 1939, Polish forces continued the fight. In France in 1940, 80,000 Polish troops were in action. The survivors regrouped in Scotland. In 1944–45 they took part in the liberation of France, Belgium and the Netherlands. Polish pilots helped the RAF in the Battle of Britain. Following Hitler's invasion of the USSR, Stalin freed Polish prisoners captured in 1939. They were allowed to leave the USSR and travel to the Middle East. Eventually more than 100,000 Poles fought against Hitler in North Africa and Italy and an equal number in northern Europe.

In 1943 the communist-led Union of Polish Patriots was established in Moscow. This eventually grew into a Polish army of more than 400,000 men fighting alongside the Soviet armies.

In Poland itself a huge 'underground' army of perhaps half-a-million grew between 1939 and 1944. As Soviet forces approached Warsaw in the summer of 1944 the Polish underground army attacked the Germans. It wanted the honour of liberating Warsaw itself although expecting Soviet help also. However, Stalin ordered the Soviet advance to halt. The Germans destroyed the Polish army and then Warsaw.

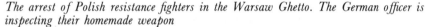

The arrest of Polish resistance fighters in the Warsaw Ghetto. The German officer is inspecting their homemade weapon

Yugoslavia

In Yugoslavia large numbers of German and Italian troops were tied down by the partisan resistance forces led by Josip Tito. In January 1943 the occupying armies planned to completely encircle and destroy Tito's forces. The partisans broke out, taking 4000 wounded with them. In a battle with the Italians they took 2000 prisoners.

Tito also fought many of his own countrymen. Some Yugoslavs in the north had joined the Ustashi who collaborated with the German invaders. Others had joined the Chetnik bands who supported the return of the Yugoslav royal family after the war. Tito and the partisans were determined that this should not happen and that the country should have a communist-led government.

The war cost the lives of one in ten Yugoslavs. Many died in the partisan fight against the invaders, others in the struggles between different groups and large numbers of civilians were killed by the Germans or Italians as reprisals for partisan sabotage or killings.

France

In France, resistance to German occupation developed between 1940 and 1942. Support for resistance groups grew with the deportation of workers to Germany and reprisals against French citizens for sabotage.

By 1943 all French resistance groups were known as the *maquis* but there were two main political groups. One was made up of communists and their left-wing allies. The others supported General Charles de Gaulle, leader of the Free French forces based in Britain.

As the *maquis* became stronger and better armed it struck more heavily against the Germans. The SS and Gestapo, aided by special French police units, struck back savagely. The worst incident was the murder of 642 people at Oradour-sur-Glane in June 1944 by an SS Division.

The *maquis* and the French 2nd Armoured Division did however have the honour of liberating their capital city on 25 August 1944 – a very different story from the fate of Warsaw.

Resistance in Germany

Opponents of Hitler

In the last free election in Germany in November 1932, the Nazi Party gained 11.7 million votes (33 per cent of the total). Once in power, Hitler's popularity increased. It is safe to say that a substantial majority of Germans supported him by 1939.

There were two important groups of Germans who did not support Hitler. The first were found among left-wingers, communists and socialists. The communists were banned early in 1933. The socialists were the only party to vote against the Enabling Law which was the basis of Hitler's dictatorship. Many communists and socialists were imprisoned for their opposition. Others fled abroad and some continued to work against Nazism from their places of exile.

The second group of opponents arose among people more usually associated with conservative views: landowners, officers and diplomats as well as some clergy. Very often they came from Prussia, the north German state which had provided most of the state officials in the old

German empire. Some opposed Hitler because they disliked the way
he had ousted them from their privileged social position but many
thought his brutal ways dishonoured Germany. Others were offended
by his treatment of the Christian churches. As the war went on,
military reasons became the strongest. To these opponents, Hitler was
leading Germany to disaster and humiliation.

**Assassination
plots**

The only way to rid Germany of Nazism was to kill Hitler. All the
leading Nazis were totally devoted to him, and would not rebel. The
armed forces had sworn an oath of personal loyalty to him. Only with
Hitler dead could a non-Nazi leader take charge and get the backing
of the Army.

There were several plots to kill Hitler. All took place after the start of
the War. Most involved soldiers, who could get hold of weapons and
explosives. The first serious attempt on Hitler's life was made by officers soon after the Stalingrad disaster. General von Treschow and Lt.
Fabian von Schlabrendorff secured a bomb disguised as two brandy

*Hitler's conference room after the explosion. The circle marks the spot where the bomb had
been placed*

bottles. They put it on Hitler's plane when he visited their head-quarters at Smolensk in the USSR. The bomb was primed to explode thirty minutes after Hitler took off. It failed. Von Schlabrendorff flew to Hitler's headquarters, coolly retrieved the bomb and dismantled it in the lavatory of a train. Several other attempts failed for various reasons, often because Hitler changed his plans at a moment's notice.

The *Abwehr*

A leading plotter against Hitler was General Hans Oster. He was a senior officer in the *Abwehr* (Military Intelligence). He used his contacts in Germany and abroad in his plans. In particular he wanted to know how the allies would treat Germany with Hitler dead. In January 1943 the allies demanded 'unconditional surrender'. This meant the plotters could expect no help from the allies.

The Kreisau Circle

Many of Hitler's most important opponents belonged to the Kreisau Circle. It was so called because they met at a country manor house in Kreisau in Silesia. They had long discussions about how Germany and Europe would be governed after Hitler.

Some of the Kreisau Circle opposed assassination. A new recruit to the conspiracy did not. He was a thirty-seven-year-old Colonel, Klaus Philip Schenk, Count von Stauffenberg. He was a courageous and gifted man with an outstanding war record. The war had also cost him an eye, a hand, and two fingers of his other hand. He had decided that Hitler's rule was an utter disaster and that he must be killed.

20 July 1944

As Chief of Staff to the Home Army, von Stauffenberg met Hitler on occasions. On 20 July 1944 he was called to a conference at Rastenburg. He entered the hut where Hitler was and placed his briefcase containing a bomb under the table. He made an excuse to leave and when he was only a short distance away the bomb exploded wrecking the hut.

Convinced that Hitler was dead, von Stauffenberg flew to Berlin. He planned to direct the takeover of the government.

Hitler survives

Hitler was not dead. Another officer had moved the briefcase to the opposite side of the heavy wooden table leg from Hitler. The blast had been directed away from him although he was hurt. It had passed through the open window of the hut. Five people were killed and nine badly injured.

The news of Hitler's survival reached Berlin before von Stauffenberg did. Four leading conspirators, including von Stauffenberg, were captured, court martialled and shot the same night.

Hitler's revenge

Hitler's escape again convinced him he had a 'divine mission'. It also led him to distrust his senior officers. Far worse was his desire for revenge. The Gestapo arrested 10,000 persons; 5000 were executed; the highest ranking officers were brought before the People's Court. On Hitler's orders they were sentenced to death by slow strangulation, hung from meat hooks on nooses of piano wire. Hitler had their executions filmed and watched their death agonies with enjoyment.

15
The Years of Defeats, 1942–45

Stalingrad and North Africa

Encirclement at Stalingrad

Stalin and his military chiefs realised that the crucial battle of the war was at Stalingrad. Fortunately for Stalin, the German advance in the form of two arrowheads left them dangerously exposed. At Stalingrad the German flanks were protected only by unreliable Romanians. By November 1942, now under the command of General Zhukov, ten Soviet armies were assembled in a huge arc of 300 kilometres. On the 19th, Zhukov ordered them to attack. Within four days, an enormous trap was sprung. 330,000 German troops were encircled. Forbidden by Hitler to surrender, then promoted to Field-Marshal, the 6th Army Commander, von Paulus, held out until 2 February 1943. Then he surrendered with his 93,000 surviving men including twenty-four generals.

Alamein

Exactly one month before Zhukov sprang the trap at Stalingrad, another important but smaller-scale allied victory began. In North Africa, under the command of General Bernard Montgomery, the British 8th Army attacked the Germans at El Alamein. Rommel's forces were driven back. Two weeks later on 7–8 November, British and American forces under US General Dwight Eisenhower landed in Morocco and Algeria. Three months after von Paulus' surrender at Stalingrad, these two allied armies, moving along the African coast met at Tunis. On 13 May 1943 more than 300,000 German and Italian troops surrendered there.

Invasion of Sicily and Italy

In July British and American forces invaded Sicily. The Italian Fascist Grand Council promptly deposed Mussolini. In September, Italy signed an armistice with the Allies. Hitler acted immediately. The German army disarmed the Italian army, rescued Mussolini and virtually took control of the country. The Allies faced a long, tough fight to capture Italy.

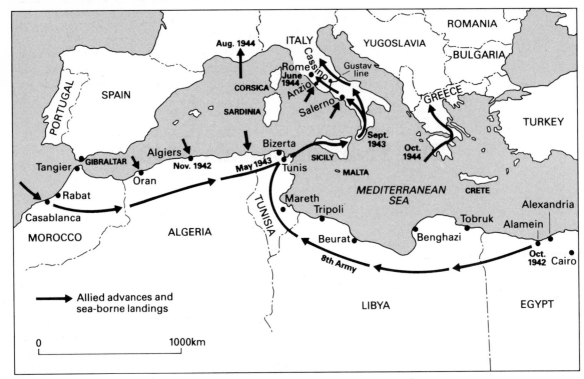

War in the Mediterranean theatre, 1942–4

The Soviet advance 1943–45

'Operation Citadel'

After Stalingrad, the Soviet Army slowly pushed the German forces back. In July 1943 Hitler decided to try for one enormous victory at Kursk. He assembled seventeen panzer divisions and almost 1 million men. The Soviet forces were 50 per cent larger with 6000 tanks against Hitler's 4500. For seven weeks the battle raged. When it was over, German power was shattered on the eastern front. In the largest tank battle in history, the USSR had proved she could outmatch the German fighting machine not only in numbers of men but in the production of tanks, aircraft and guns.

Leningrad relieved

Following the huge victory at Kursk, the Soviet army advanced on all fronts. It had 5.5 million men against less than 4 million Germans. The long seige of Leningrad was ended early in 1944. By the spring, Soviet forces were preparing to enter Poland, Czechoslovakia and Romania.

D-Day

Operation Overlord

From 1942–44 hundreds of thousands of US sailors, soldiers and airmen arrived in Britain. The sailors were mainly involved in the Battle of the Atlantic against the U-boats. Many also sailed with the invasion fleet to North Africa in November 1942. The US airmen began increasingly heavy daylight bombing attacks on Germany. The RAF had been flying by night since 1940. The US soldiers were preparing, alongside equal numbers of British and Canadian forces, for the invasion of western Europe. This was codenamed 'Overlord'.

Dieppe

In August 1942 the Allies had made a seaborne attack on the French channel port of Dieppe. It was heavily defended. The attackers, mostly Canadians, were massacred. The Allied generals realised that when D-Day came there would be one chance only. The attack would have to be planned and launched in total secrecy. However, it would have to be on a very large scale. The Germans had sixty divisions waiting in France.

Montgomery and Eisenhower

At the end of 1943 General Montgomery was brought back from Italy and put in command of the invasion forces. General Eisenhower was appointed overall Allied Commander.

The landings were planned to be on five beaches in Normandy. However the Germans were deceived into believing the real attack would take place near Calais. D-Day was 6 June 1944. Over 200,000 Allied men took part. The Germans thought it was a feint. By the time they realised it was the real thing, it was too late to dislodge the Allies.

Men of a wartime labour brigade making part of the 'Atlantic Wall' to defend German-occupied France, Belgium and Holland from attack by sea

Within 10 days a million men had landed in France. Hitler's reply was to launch V–I rockets on South-east England. These were fast, pilot-less bombs carrying a one-ton warhead. 8000 fell on London, killing 5000 people and injuring 40,000 more. The fifteen-metre-long V-2 rocket also carried a war-head of one ton. More than a thousand of these were launched against London and other targets in the autumn and winter of 1944–45.

Paris liberated

Stalin helped the Western Allies by launching a huge offensive in the east. The German army was now outnumbered heavily on both fronts in both men and weapons. In France it was losing an average of 2500 men daily and could not replace these losses.

After heavy fighting, the Allied armies advanced south and east. Paris was liberated by French forces on 25 August and British forces freed Brussels on 2 September.

'A bridge too far'

As the advance continued, the Allied forces spread across an everwidening front. Germany's defences were weakest in the north near the Dutch border. The Allies decided to use 1st Airborne Army to seize three important river bridges in Holland. These would give Allied forces a route directly into Germany as they linked up with the paratroopers. Unfortunately the third vital bridge over the Rhine at Arnhem could not be captured by the British 1st Airborne Division. It landed amongst strong German forces and suffered 60 per cent casualties.

The Battle of the Bulge

By December the Allied advance had come to a halt. Hitler thought that they were close to defeat. He gathered twenty-eight divisions, his last reserves, and attacked on 16 December. Allied fighter planes were grounded by fog. The German advance broke through the US lines aiming for Antwerp. Then the Allies struck back. By early January the Germans were retreating. This failure cost Hitler 120,000 men and 600 tanks.

The collapse of Nazi Germany

Warsaw captured

A few days after Hitler broke off his offensive in the west, the Soviet army attacked in the east. On 12 January 1945 an enormous threepronged attack began, involving 180 Soviet divisions. By now the Germans were outnumbered five to two on the eastern front. The Soviet army moved forward over-running all German defences. Warsaw was captured on 17 January. By mid-February, Budapest had fallen and the advance forces were within 100 kilometres of Berlin. The Germans had suffered another 500,000 casualties.

Rhine crossing

In the west, eighty-five Allied divisions advanced to the Rhine. The first crossing by Americans was at Remagen on 7 March. Further north a huge force under Montgomery crossed on 23 March and began advancing on Bremen and Hamburg. By 11 April US forces were within 100 kilometres of Berlin. On 16th Zhukov launched the final attack on Berlin and on 25th US and Soviet forces met at Torgau. Further south, Vienna was captured by the Soviet army on 12 April but Prague was not taken until 9 May.

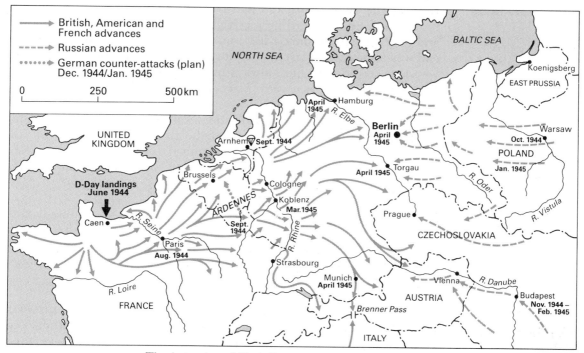

The destruction of Nazi Germany, 1944–5

The bunker

Hitler had spent most of the War since June 1941 at his eastern headquarters at Rastenburg in East Prussia. He left there on 20 November 1944 as the Soviet army advanced. On 16 January 1945 he retreated into his bunker 15 metres underground in Berlin. His original plan was to leave Berlin on his birthday, 20 April. Then he would make his 'last stand' at the Berghof in the Alps. This was not to happen.

The Allied advances on Berlin and elsewhere met little resistance.

Death of Roosevelt

On 12 April, President Roosevelt died. Goebbels and some of the Nazis believed that somehow this would save Germany from defeat. Hitler said the Soviet army would be totally defeated in Berlin. By the 22nd, as Soviet units began surrounding the city, Hitler decided he would stay in Berlin and die there.

Göring arrested

Göring, Himmler and Ribbentrop all fled from Berlin on 20 April. Three days later, Göring sent a telegram from southern Germany to Hitler. He suggested he should take over the leadership of Germany if Hitler had lost his 'freedom of action'. A few hours later the SS arrested Göring.

Himmler also believed Hitler would soon be dead. He met Count Bernadotte, the Swedish Consul in Lubeck. He tried to persuade him to call Eisenhower to discuss a German surrender in the west. Then, said Himmler, the British and Americans would join with the Germans in attacking the Soviet army!

Hitler's wedding

Even at this time Hitler still had fantasies of a relief army coming to rescue him. On 28 April he received the news of Himmler's treachery and of Soviet troops only a few hundred metres away. Hitler knew the end was approaching fast and wanted to repay the loyalty of Eva Braun who had stayed with him, always in the background, for fifteen years. Early on 29 April they were married by a Berlin city councillor.

Hitler's will

Hitler then drafted his last will and testament. He sought to justify everything he had done. He blamed the British and, most of all, the Jews for starting the War. He condemned the leaders of the armed forces and the SS who had 'betrayed him' and expelled Göring and Himmler from the NSDAP.

Death of Mussolini

Later the same day (29 April) Hitler learned that his fellow dictator Mussolini and his mistress Clara Petacci had been captured and shot. Their bodies had been strung up and then left in a gutter for several hours. Hitler had already decided that the bodies of Eva and himself were to be burnt after their deaths.

Death of Hitler

Hitler said goodbye to his staff. He and Eva retired to their quarters. Two shots were heard. Goebbels and some others entered the room. It was 3.30 p.m. on Monday 30 April 1945.

The bodies were carried outside and placed in a shell hole. Hitler's chauffeur had collected 180 litres of petrol and he poured it over the bodies and set them alight. Twenty-four hours later Goebbels and his wife poisoned their six children; an SS man then shot the couple at their own request. Several hundred survivors from the bunker began a mass break-out through the Soviet lines. Some succeeded.

Surrender

On 29 April the German armies in Italy surrendered unconditionally. On 4 May all German forces in north-west Germany surrendered to Montgomery. Finally on 7 May General Jodl and Admiral Hans von Friedeburg signed a full unconditional surrender at General Eisenhower's headquarters in Reims, France.

The war ended at midnight on 8 May 1945 and Nazi Germany ceased to exist.

16
Germany and Europe in 1945

The toll

50 million plus

The death total in the Second World War exceeded 50 million. This included 10 million Chinese and 3 million Japanese in the war in the Far East. In Europe the 20 million Soviet citizens killed were 38 per cent of *all* Second World War deaths. They exceeded *all* the deaths of the rest of Europe *combined*. Millions of the Soviet dead were prisoners and ethnic minorites killed on Stalin's orders by Soviet forces.

Germany with 6.8 million, Poland 6.2 (mostly Jews) and Yugoslavia 1.7 million, had the next greatest death tolls. Even countries which collapsed quickly after the German attack suffered heavy losses. These included 800,000 French citizens killed, 400,000 Czechs, 520,000 Greeks and 210,000 Dutch.

By contrast Britain and the USA, both involved in heavy fighting, lost 'only' 400,000 each killed. Canada (34,000) and Australia (12,000) escaped lightly. In total, however, the Germans and their allies lost only one person killed for every four in the victorious nations.

Bombing

Compared with the almost total destruction of Hiroshima and Nagasaki by atomic bombs in August 1945, most European cities suffered less. However a number of European cities were almost totally destroyed by bombing and artillery fire. These included Warsaw, Leningrad, Belgrade, Dresden, Berlin, Brest and Le Havre.

Overall the greatest damage was done in the USSR, Poland and Germany. Vast quantities of housing were destroyed. So were dams, harbours, bridges, railways, factories, and power stations. By 1945 European industry was producing one-third of the 1938 total.

Food shortages

Agricultural production had fallen by about half. This was the result of huge armies fighting across farmlands, millions of farm workers being conscripted into armies, and shortages of farm machinery. Severe hunger and famine in places was the fate of many Europeans in 1945.

In total the war cost 25 per cent of the USSR's capital assets (buildings, machinery, roads, railways and so on), 18 per cent of Britain's and 10 per cent of France's.

Displaced persons   The war had uprooted countless millions from their homes in addition to soldiers who had to fight in distant lands and civilians who went to work in war industries. The greatest disruptions were in eastern Europe among those transported to slave factories and extermination camps. Additionally millions fled westwards to escape the vengeance of the Soviet army. Many were German people who had lived pre-war in Poland, Hungary and Yugoslavia. Others were from groups who had fought for the Germans against the Communists in the USSR.

In 1945 central Europe was teeming with millions of 'displaced persons'. The great majority were housed in camps until they could be resettled. The fortunate ones found new lives in Israel, Britain, Canada, the USA or Australia. The worst fate was that of Soviet army prisoners who had often joined the German army to escape death by starvation. They were handed back to Stalin at bayonet point.

The political scene

Europe reduced   Germany and France were defeated and devastated in 1945. Britain possessed the world's second largest navy and bomber force and an army spread across the world, larger than Hitler's which attacked the USSR in 1941. Yet, Britain was almost totally exhausted and close to bankruptcy. In the last year or two of the war the government had been spending £16 million *per day* (equal to £225 million in 1990). Additionally, Britain had received £30 billion in US aid.

The super-powers   The USSR was also battered and exhausted. However, its huge army had destroyed Hitler's, inflicting 10 million casualties upon it. Soviet troops occupied almost all of eastern Europe. In the next few years communist governments would take power in all these countries. The USSR had emerged from the War as a super-power.

So also had the USA, the second and far stronger super-power. In 1939 much of US industry had been lying idle. There were 7 million Americans unemployed. The war created new factories, shipyards, coalmines and oil wells. The USA was able not only to supply its own enormous armed forces of 12.5 million men – for example 96,000 war planes were built in 1944 – vast quantities of munitions were also sent to Britain and the USSR. Yet this burden was carried *without* exhausting the economy. By the end of the war, US gold reserves had risen from $20 billion to $33 billion. The total production of US wealth rose from $88 billion in 1938 to $220 billion in 1945.

Thus in 1945 the two super-powers, the USA and the USSR, faced each other across a divided, devastated, and greatly weakened Europe.

This was Hitler's legacy.

Nuremburg

Hitler was dead; Goebbels was dead; Heydrich was long dead. Himmler committed suicide on 23 May 1945 when captured by British troops.

Hess had already been in captivity for four years after having flown secretly to Scotland in May 1941. Göring was also captured. These last two and nineteen others were brought to Nuremburg in November 1945 and placed on trial. They were charged with 'crimes against humanity' and waging an aggressive war.

The judges

The British Judge Lord Justice Lawrence was president of a panel of nine judges from the four major victorious powers. A judge from the US Supreme Court was the Chief Prosecutor. For eleven months an enormous quantity of evidence from witnesses and from documents piled up. Göring was proud of his position of chief defendant. Hess appeared to have lost his memory. Speer was honest and hid nothing.

The verdicts

Three were acquitted – von Papen, Dr Schacht and Hans Fritzsche of German Radio. Seven were jailed; Hess, for life, dying in Spandau Prison, Berlin, in 1987, at the age of ninety-three. Speer served twenty years, being released in 1966. Eleven were sentenced to death. Göring committed suicide two hours before his execution. The remaining ten were hanged in the early hours of 16 October 1946.

'National Socialism', wrote Alan Bullock, 'produced nothing. The sole theme of the Nazi revolution was domination dressed up as the doctrine of race and failing that a vindictive destructiveness. It is this emptiness, the lack of anything to justify the suffering he caused ... which makes Hitler so repellent and so barren a figure.'

The last photograph of Hitler. He is congratulating boys who took part in the last defence of Berlin

Index

(Major topics such as Hitler, Germany and the Nazi Party are not listed in the index because of their great frequency. They can, however, be traced through the Contents, pages 3–5)

Abyssinia, 85
Africa, North, 115, 118, 135
Afrika Korps, 118
Alliances and Pacts, Anglo-German Naval, 85; Anglo-Polish, 104–8; Anti-Comintern, 87–8; Berlin, 41; Franco-Polish, 107; Franco-Russian, 15; Franco-Soviet, 85, 100; Japanese-Soviet, 116; Kellogg-Briand, 91; Locarno, 41, 86; Nazi-Polish, 83, 105; Nazi-Soviet, 107; Pact of Steel, 107; Soviet-Czech, 85; Triple Alliance, 15; Triple Entente, 15
Alsace and Lorraine, 21, 32, 107
Amann, Max, 37
Anschluss, Der, 90–3
Anti-Semitism, *see* Jews
Army, German, 15–19, 20–1, 23, 53, 54–7, 62, 67–8, 76–8, 84–5, 87–141
Auschwitz camp, 128–9
Austria, 9, 22, 27, 36, 38, 82–4, 89, 90–3, 121
Austro-Hungarian Empire, 9–13, 18, 21, 22, 36, 82, 105, 142

Baltic States, 23, 24, 31, 82, 108–9, 129
Battle of Britain, 114
Bavaria, 13–14, 19, 24–31, 33–7, 38–40, 43, 53–4, 56–7, 72
Beck Col. J., 105
Beer-Hall putsch, 33–6
Berlin, 19, 20, 28, 39, 47, 54–5, 65, 72, 74, 95, 98, 101, 102, 107, 108, 114, 127, 134, 138–40
Bismarck, Count Otto von, 15
Blomberg, F-M. W. von, 68, 88
Bock, F-M. W. von, 117
Bormann, Martin, 67
Boulher, Philip, 124
Brauchitsh, F-M. W. von 68

Braun, Eva, 42, 140
Britain, 15, 24, 41, 56, 82, 82–120, 135–144
Brüning, Heinrich, 44, 47, 50

Canaris, Adml. W., 74
Chamberlain, Neville, 95–100, 104–5, 112
Centre Party, 14, 44, 46, 51, 53, 55
Churches, German, 66, 67, 125, 132–3
Churchill, Winston, 100, 112, 114
Clemenceau, Georges, 20
Communist Party of Germany, 19, 34, 46–7, 50, 51, 53–5, 132
Concentration camps, 74–6, 80
Courts, German Law, 53, 78–80, 134
Czechoslovakia, 9, 22, 23, 24, 27, 82, 89, 93–103, 104, 105, 109, 136

D-Day, 136–8
Daladier, Edouard, 96, 99, 100
Dawes, Charles, 40
De Gaulle, Charles, 132
Depression, World Economic, 42–44
Diels, Dr Rudolf, 54, 72
Dietrich, Sepp., 76
Dollfuss, Engelbert, 84, 90
Drexler, Anton, 25
Dunkirk evacuation, 112

Ebert, Frederick, 19, 20, 40
Eckhart, Dietrich, 27–8, 32
Economy, German, 15, 20, 32, 40–1, 43, 53, 59–63, 88–9, 91, 101, 121–3
Education, German, 70–1, 76, 77—8
Eicke, Theodore, 74, 75
Eisenhower, Gen.D.D., 135, 137, 140

Eisner, Kurt, 19, 24
El Alamein, 118, 135
Elections, German, 14, 19, 38, 40, 41, 44, 46–51, 54, 86, 132
Enabling Law, 55, 132
Euthanasia programme, 123–5
Extermination camps, 127–9

Final solution, *see* Jews
Finland, 23, 110
France, 15, 23, 24, 32, 40–1, 56, 82–141
Franco, Gen.F., 87
Frank, Anne, 6–8
Franz Josef II, 10
Frick, Wilhelm, 58, 72
Fritsch, Gen. W. von, 68, 77, 88

Galen, Archbp. C. von, 66, 125
German Workers' Party, 24–7, 31
Gestapo, 8, 72–5, 93, 126
Goebbels, Dr Joseph, 39, 58, 65, 80–1, 109, 111, 139, 140, 143
Göring, F-M. Hermann, 31, 34, 36, 58, 62, 65, 68, 72, 79, 88, 94, 139, 140, 143
Graf, Ulrich, 34, 36
Groener, Gen., 19
Gypsies, 74, 126, 127, 129

Hacha, Pres., 102
Halifax, Lord, 104
Hanisch, Reinhardt, 10
Harrer, Dietrich, 24
Hausser, Gen.P., 76
Heiden, Konrad, 41
Henderson, Sir Neville, 97, 104–5
Henlein, Konrad, 94, 96, 113
Hess, Rudolf, 32, 36, 143
Heydrich, Reinhardt, 56, 72, 73, 74, 75, 126, 127, 143